Ken Schessler's
This is
Hollywood

"Fielding and Frommer — flake off! Jack Smith — bite your Big Orange! Ken Schessler has probably created the ultimate Los Angeles Guide book, the best yet to a city that has been without a first-rate handbook that captures its local color."

—Jules Minton, San Fernando Valley Express

"The book that shows you the real Hollywood."

—P.M. Magazine

"The most imitated guide book ever published!"
—Dewey Webb — Arizona New-Times

"The ONLY guide to Hollywood. Unbelievable research!
—Paul Wallach, KIEV Radio

"The best guide in Los Angeles."

—Cleve Hermann, KFWB Radio

"Reveals a side of Hollywood that few tourists or locals ever see."
—Cleveland Plain Dealer

"Ken Schessler uncovers a Hollywood you will never forget."
—20/20 Magazine

"THIS IS HOLLYWOOD is the only way to see Hollywood."
—Wall Street Journal

Printing History

First printing, August 1978   Seventh printing, April 1988
Second printing, November 1979   Eighth printing, January 1989
Third printing, October 1980   Ninth printing, August 1989
Fourth printing, February 1983   Tenth printing, March 1991
Fifth printing, January 1984   Eleventh printing, January 1993
Sixth printing, March 1987   Twelfth Printing, August 1995
           Fourteenth Printing, January 1997

ISBN 0-915633-00-0
Library of Congress Catalog Card Number 86-090678

Published by
Ken Schessler Publishing   P.O. Box 7800
Redlands, CA 92375
909-798-2243

PRINTED IN THE UNITED STATES OF AMERICA

Ken Schessler's

This is
Hollywood

An Unusual
Guide

By
Ken Schessler

TO EVELYN

Without whose help this book would have never been written

The photographs in this book were made by the author
or are from his private collection.

Maps by the author

DISCOVER THE REAL
HOLLYWOOD

To most people, Hollywood is what they see on the surface —Mann's Grauman's Chinese Theatre, Universal Studios, and Hollywood and Vine. But underneath these tourist attractions there is much, much more to the world's most famous city than meets the eye of the average tourist or local resident.

First of all, Hollywood is not just the area centered around Hollywood & Vine. Its undefined boundaries are vast, extending from the San Fernando Valley, to the Pacific Ocean. Since the birth of the movies in Los Angeles in 1909, Hollywood's fabled pioneers and stars have not only left their imprints in the forecourt of Grauman's Chinese, but in countless other places in the Los Angeles area where the Hollywood history buff and explorer, or just plain fan, can find exciting history at every turn.

Beginning in the early sixties, Hollywood's fabulous history, like that of Rome was being neglected—even buried. Until *THIS IS HOLLYWOOD,* Hollywood had been without a first-rate guide book that revealed its golden past—one that truly had the color and flavor of the REAL Hollywood, something besides foot and handprints and sidewalk stars—something different.

When Ken Schessler researched and wrote *THIS IS HOLLYWOOD,* he created Los Angeles' and Hollywood's most interesting and unusual guide book. It is the only guide that takes you to the little known and unusual sites such as the spot where Hollywood was founded, where the first movie was made, Hollywood's first night club, to famous homes such as Errol Flynn's "Mulholland House" where he had one-way mirrors installed in the bedroom ceilings, homes where Marilyn Monroe, Sharon Tate, and John Belushi died, and even homes that are reportedly "haunted" by famous stars. It guides you to the sites of all of Hollywood's scandals, murders and graves of the stars.

This unusual and exciting guide will help you discover a Hollywood that you never knew existed—from its historical beginnings, through over eighty years of movie history. It takes you behind the tinsel, down dingy side streets and to the mansions of Beverly Hills. Just reading the fascinating stories in this book will be an experience you will never forget.

CENTRAL HOLLYWOOD

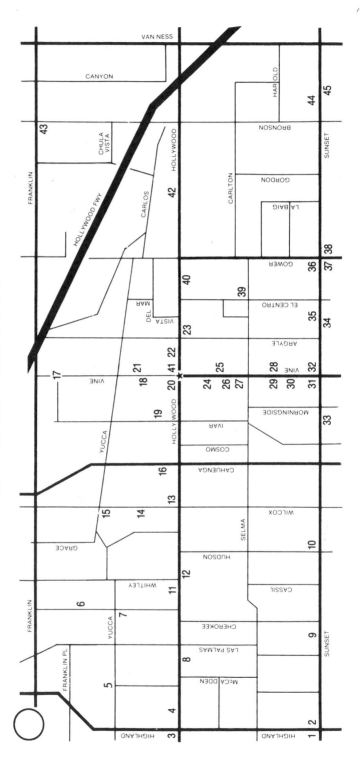

CENTRAL HOLLYWOOD

Sunset Boulevard entrance to Hollywood High School

1.   Hollywood High School. Lana Turner, Carol Burnett, Rick and David Nelson, Stefanie Powers, Bishop James J. Pike and Norman Chandler, are just a few of this school's famous graduates. The school nickname is the "Shiek's." 1521 N. Highland.

2.   Lana Turner Discovered in Malt Shop. Despite all that has been written about Lana being discovered at Schwab's, she was really found here in an ice cream shop across from Hollywood High in 1936. A mini-mall is now on the site. 1500 N. Highland.

3.   Hollywood's First Hotel. Built in 1903, The Hollywood Hotel was the home of many celebrities. In 1919, Rudolph Valentino's first wife, Jean Acker, locked him out of their honeymoon suite here. Carrie Jacobs Bond wrote her famous song "The End of a Perfect Day" while living here in the hotel. Destroyed in 1957, the site is now a bank and parking lot. 6811 Hollywood Blvd.

4.   Hollywood's First Night Club. The creaky old stairs here will take you up to the second floor where the Montmartre Cafe was opened in 1923. On any given day one could see Valentino dancing with Pola Negri, or Charlie Chaplin wooing Marion Davies. In 1925, Joan Crawford never missed the Wednesday lunch dances. Bing Crosby was a regular performer here. 6757 Hollywood Blvd.

5.   James Dean's Favorite Hangout. It was here at the Villa Capri Restaurant that Dean had dinner the night before he was killed in an auto accident in 1955. He always entered and left through the kitchen. A favorite meeting place of the "Rat Pack" which included members Humphrey Bogart, Frank Sinatra, Sammy Davis Jr., Lauren Bacall and Judy Garland, the building has been the home of an FM radio station in recent years. 6735 Yucca.

6.   Home of the Black Dahlia. Elizabeth Short, the "Black Dahlia," was living here in an apartment in September 1946, four months before she was murdered. 1842 N. Cherokee.

7. Wizard of Oz's "Ozcot." In 1909, L. Frank Baum, author of *The Wizard of Oz* built his home on this site. It was here that he wrote many of his famous children's books and where he grew dahlias and chrysanthemums that won him honors in local flower shows. "Ozcot," as Baum called his estate, contained an aviary of several hundred birds, and an archery range. Baum's beloved "Ozcot" was destroyed in the 1950s when apartments were constructed on the site. In his books, Baum always described "Oz" as being surrounded by the Deadly Desert on the west, the Great Sandy Waste on the south, the Impassable Desert on the north, and the Shifting Sands on the east. When he died here in 1919 after being in a coma for twenty-four hours, Baum was reported to have spoken only once during that time. A minute before he died he said quite distinctly, "Now we can cross the shifting sands." 1749 N. Cherokee.

8. Hollywood's First Movie Premiere. Built in 1922 by Sid Grauman, the Egyptian Theatre opened up with Hollywood's first premiere. The film was *Robin Hood* and starred Douglas Fairbanks Sr., Wallace Beery and Alan Hale. 6708 Hollywood Blvd.

9. L.A.'s First Outdoor Shopping Mall. The Crossroads of the World opened in 1936 and featured unusual shaped shops of Spanish, French and Italian architecture. 6671 Sunset Blvd.

10. Hollywood's Tower of Babylon. The former Hollywood Athletic Club, built in 1923, was a favorite of male stars during the 1920s thru the 50s. John Barrymore and John Wayne used the ninth floor penthouse rooms for their drinking parties. Ramon Novarro used the same rooms for trysts with his many lovers. Valentino stayed here whenever he had a disagreement with one of his wives. The restored structure still contains the olympic sized pool that once held the likes of Clark Gable, Robert Taylor and John Gilbert. In 1931, silent screen star Tyrone Power Sr., died here in his room in the arms of his 17 year-old son, Tyrone, Jr. 6525 Sunset Blvd.

11. Hollywood's Oldest Restaurant. Musso & Frank's has been in Hollywood since 1919. The backroom during the 1930s and 40s, was the hangout for such writers as William Faulkner, Raymond Chandler, Nathanael West and William Saroyan. 6667 Hollywood.

12. Fredericks of Hollywood. 6608 Hollywood Boulevard.

13. Woman Who Gave Hollywood its Name. Mrs. Daeida (Wilcox) Beveridge, known as "The Mother of Hollywood," died here in her home in 1914. Mrs. Wilcox and her first husband, Horace H. Wilcox, founded Hollywood in 1887. The name "Hollywood" was first brought to Mrs. Wilcox' attention while talking to a woman on the train during a trip back east. The lady often spoke of her country home, Hollywood. The name so pleased Mrs. Wilcox, that when she returned to Los Angeles, she too, named her home "Hollywood." Over one-hundred years later, Hollywood has yet to honor Mrs. Wilcox in anyway. A bank is now on the site. 6467 Hollywood.

CENTRAL HOLLYWOOD

The Dolly Sisters (Jenny on left)   Clara Blandick

14.   Suicide Hotel. The Shelton Apartments was the scene of two of Hollywood's most tragic suicides, Jenny Dolly in 1941, and Clara Blandick in 1962. Identical twins, "The Dolly Sisters," Jenny and Rosie, were a world famous dancing team in the early 1900s. They were the toast of two continents—two of the most beautiful women in the world. Legend has it that Jenny was the only woman ever to break the bank at Monte Carlo. Friends said that Jenny lived under a doom and a spell. In 1933, she was disfigured in an auto accident—operations left her once beautiful face scarred. Jenny would tell acquaintances, "The doctors didn't do me any favors by saving my life." In 1941, Jenny was found dead in her living room here. She had hanged herself with a bright-hued sash from a wrought iron curtain rod in a window that looked up to the Hollywood Hills.

Twenty-one years later, actress Clara Blandick killed herself in her apartment yards from where Jenny Dolly was found. Miss Blandick is best remembered for her role as Judy Garland's "Auntie Em" in *The Wizard of Oz*. Miss Blandick dressed herself in an elegant royal blue gown, primped her hair, checked her make-up, lay down on the couch, pulled a gold colored blanket up over her shoulders, then being careful not to muss her hair, she slipped a plastic bag over her head. The Shelton was torn down in 1987. 1735 N. Wilcox.

Shelton apartments where Jenny Dolly and Clara Blandick died.

CENTRAL HOLLYWOOD

15. Fernwood Flasher Murdered. One-half block up the street from where Jenny Dolly and Clara Blandick died is the apartment

Victor Kilian

building where actor Victor Kilian was murdered in 1979. (The Lido apartments where he lived can be seen on the right in the photo on page 9). Kilian, who had appeared in over 140 films, portrayed the crazy uncle, "The Fernwood Flasher," in the TV series *Mary Hartman, Mary Hartman*. He was beaten to death here in his apartment while watching television. He was 88 years old. 6500 Yucca St.

16. Site of Hollywood's Birthplace. Horace H. Wilcox and his wife Daeida founded Hollywood in 1887. It was this site on Cahuenga Blvd. that Mrs. Wilcox gave the name "Hollywood." In 1901, Mrs. Wilcox sold the original home and grounds to Paul DeLongpre, a famous French flower artist. The palatial home and beautiful flower gardens were Hollywood's first tourist attraction. No plaque marks the site, which is now a parking lot. The only thing in Hollywood that bears the Wilcox name is Wilcox Ave. which Wilcox, who died in 1891, named himself. 1721 N. Cahuenga.

17. Silent Star Kills Self With Scissors. Lou Tellegen was one of Hollywood's biggest stars in the 1920s—a matinee idol with millions of fans all over the world. When sound films were introduced, he, like many others, became an instant "has-been." In 1934, despondent, his career finished, he decided to end his life with a dramatic flair while a guest in the Cudahy mansion near Hollywood and Vine. Locking himself in his bathroom, he carefully shaved and powdered his once handsome face. Then while standing in front of a full length mirror, he stabbed himself in the heart seven times with a pair of sewing scissors. When his former wife, opera star

Lou Tellegen

Geraldine Farrar, was notified of his death, she replied, "I am not interested in the least." His wife at the time, sent her regrets from New York. Only thirty-seven friends and fans showed up for his funeral. He was 53 years old. The Vine/Franklin underpass of the Hollywood freeway now covers the site. 1844 N. Vine.

18. Hollywood Palace. Opened in 1927 as the Hollywood Playhouse it later became the El Capitan in 1942, and the Hollywood Palace in 1964. *Ken Murray's Blackouts, This is Your life,* and many other shows emanated from here. 1735 N. Vine.

19. Designer Irene Leaps to Her Death. Leaving a suicide note apologizing to other guests of the Knickerbocker Hotel, motion picture dress designer, "Irene" (depressed by financial problems, and her husband's illness) jumped from the top floor of the hotel to her death on the lobby roof in 1962. She was 60 years old. The hotel, built in 1925, is now a retirement home. 1714 N. Ivar.

20. Sardi's. World famous in the 1930s and 40s, and originally known as Henry's Cafe & Deli. Charlie Chaplin was a regular diner here. It has been a porno theatre in recent years. 6315 Hollywood.

21. Capitol Records Tower. The world's first circular office building was built in 1956 by singer Johnny Mercer. 1750 N. Vine.

22. Hollywood's Most Beautiful Theatre. Opened in 1930, the Pantages Theatre was the host to the Academy Awards from 1949 to 1959. Howard Hughes once had offices here. 6233 Hollywood.

23. Mortuary of the Stars. The funeral services of many stars were held here at the former W.M. Strothers Mortuary including Peg Entwistle, Wallace Reid, Tom Ince, Bela Lugosi, June Mathis, and wrestler Gorgeous George. 6240 Hollywood.

24. Clara Bow's It Cafe. Actress Clara Bow and her husband Rex Bell opened up the "It" Cafe here off the lobby of the Plaza Hotel in 1943. Built in 1925, the Plaza is now a retirement home. 1637 Vine.

25. Brown Derby Restaurant of the Stars. The Brown Derby, opened on Valentines Day in 1929. It was here in 1939 that Clark Gable purposed to Carole Lombard. Closed in 1985, most of the Derby was destroyed by fire in 1988. 1628 N. Vine.

26. Mike Lyman's Grill. Originally called "Al Levy's," Lyman's was one of Hollywood's popular restaurants in the 1940s. The site is now a parking lot. 1623 N. Vine.

27. Huntington Hartford Theatre. Built in 1927 as the Wilkes Vine St. Theatre, it later became the Queen Theatre. In 1932 it was the Mirror Theatre, and in the late 1930s and early 1940s it was the CBS Playhouse Theatre where Cecil B. DeMille presented the *Lux Radio Theatre*. It became the Huntington Hartford in 1954 and was renamed the Doolittle Theatre in 1985. 1615 N. Vine.

28. Rudolph Valentino's Home Studio. In 1913, Jesse Lasky and Cecil B. DeMille made Hollywood's first full length picture *The Squaw Man* here on the site of the Famous Players-Lasky Studio. Valentino made most of his pictures here. Torn down in the 1930s, the Hollywood Palladium, a bank, an office building and parking lot now cover the site. The original barn/studio is now a museum across from the Hollywood Bowl (See page 36). 1521 N. Vine.

29. Bowling Alley Now TV Studios. Known as the Tom Brenneman Bowling Lanes in the 1940s, and converted into a TV studio by Merv Griffin in the 70s. Now ABC Studios. 1541 Vine.

30.   Breakfast in Hollywood Restaurant. A popular radio show during the 1940s hosted by Tom Brenneman, was broadcast from here every morning. In 1940 it was the Tropics Restaurant. The building was destroyed in 1982 for a mini-mall. 1525 Vine.

31.   Wallich's Music City. Opened in 1940 and billed as having the world's largest serve-yourself record department, Wallich's was the first to seal record albums in cellophane and to put them in self-service display racks. Regular weekly customers included Frank Sinatra, Mary Pickford and Fred Astaire. In 1982, Wallich's was destroyed for a parking lot and mini-mall. 1501 N. Vine.

32.   NBC Radio Studios. The NBC Radio Studios were located here in the 40s and 50s. Many radio shows including the Jack Benny and Bob Hope shows originated here. Destroyed in the 1960s, a bank is now on the site. 1500 N. Vine.

33.   Cinerama Dome Theatre. Built in 1963. 6360 Sunset.

34.   The Most Beautiful Girls in the World. The Earl Carroll Theatre opened on Christmas Day in 1938. W.C. Fields and Jack Benny helped break ground for its construction. With a cast of 60 gorgeous girls on stage, opening night was the most dazzling event ever in the night life of Hollywood. Every star of any importance attended. The legendary theatre had the first double revolving stages ever constructed, 90 feet in circumference—the largest in the world. The neon sign above the entrance proclaimed, "Through these portals pass the most beautiful girls in the world." Carroll and his girl friend, Beryl Wallace, the star of the show, were killed in a plane crash in 1948. Called the Moulin Rouge in 1953, later it was a night club for teenagers, and in recent years it has been the Aquarius Theatre where the TV show *Star Search* was filmed in 1992. 6230 Sunset.

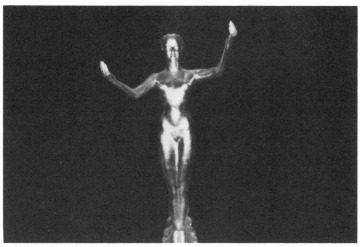

Nude Statue of Earl Carroll star stands in theatre lobby.

CENTRAL HOLLYWOOD

35.   Hollywood Palladium. Built in 1940 by Los Angeles Times publisher, Norman Chandler, the Palladium, with its huge dance floor played host to all the big bands during the 1940s and 50s. Lawrence Welk appeared here weekly for almost fifteen years. In the early 1920s the site was an outdoor movie set on the backlot of the Famous Players-Lasky movie studio. 6215 Sunset.

36.   Hollywood's First Movie Studio. In 1911, Al Christie and David Horsley of the Nestor Film Company rented a tavern and barn here and started Hollywood's first studio. In 1912, Nestor merged with Universal Studios. In 1915, it became the Christie Studios where comedies were filmed. In 1938, CBS built Columbia Square on the site. It is now CBS TV channel 2. 6101 Sunset.

37.   Original Universal Studios. Owned by Universal in 1912, it later became the LKO Studio. In 1918 the Stern Brothers renamed it the Century Studios. Ill-fated actress Virginia Rappe, who died in the infamous "Fatty" Arbuckle case, worked at this studio at the time of her tragic death in 1921. The site is now a mini-mall. 6100 Sunset.

Gower Gulch, 1920s hangout for cowboy extras.

38.   Gower Gulch/Poverty Row. In the early 1920s, this corner of Sunset and Gower was the hangout for "movie cowboys" who waited here in hopes of being picked for "extra work" in the westerns that were filmed in studios nearby. The corner was named "Gower Gulch." The street and nearby area were known as "Poverty Row" because of the small studios that were located here. 6098 Sunset.

39.   Hollywood Legion Stadium. From the 1920s to the 50s, the Legion Stadium was THE place to go on Friday night—it was fight night. Built in 1923, the arena featured such fighters as James J. Braddock and Joe Louis. Regular weekly customers were Rudolph Valentino, Charlie Chaplin, Jean Harlow, George Raft, Clark Gable and Carole Lombard. In 1960, the arena was filled in with concrete and the stadium became a bowling alley. In 1986, the former fight arena was turned into a reducing salon. 1628 El Centro.

40. Hollywood's First Movie. When producer Al Christie of the Nestor Film Company arrived in Hollywood in 1911, he rented property on Sunset Blvd. The next day, Christie took his small troupe out into the orange groves north of the property and filmed Hollywood's first movie. Christie later bought the groves and in 1925, on the exact spot where he filmed the first movie, he built the Regent Hotel. Called the Hastings in recent years. 6162 Hollywood.

41. Ghost of Lon Chaney Seen at Hollywood & Vine. In 1913, when actor Lon Chaney was still an extra, he used to sit on a bench on the corner of Hollywood and Vine and wait for transportation that would take him to the studios. When he became a star, he would drive by the same bench and pick up the movie extras who were waiting for transportation. After Chaney died in 1930, his ghost was reported seen sitting on the bench. Finally, a spot was reserved for the ghost and nobody ever sat on it. When the bench was replaced with a new one in 1942, his ghost was never seen again. NE corner Hollywood/Vine.

42. Marilyn Monroe's First Wedding. During the 1940s, the Florentine Gardens featured such headliners as Sophie Tucker, and Ozzie Nelson. Managed by Nils Thor Granlund, the chorus of beautiful girls at one time included Yvonne De Carlo, Marie McDonald, Gwen Verdon and Lily St. Cyr. In 1942, Marilyn Monroe and her first husband celebrated their wedding here. Milton Berle held his wedding reception here. 5951 Hollywood.

43. Hollywood's Most Beautiful Building. The Chateau Elysee Apartments were built in 1929 on the site of producer Tom Ince's first home. Ince died mysteriously in 1924 after being a guest on the yacht of William Randolph Hearst. Other guests on the yacht at the time Ince "took sick" were actress Marion Davies and comedian Charlie Chaplin. To this day, rumors persist that Hearst shot and killed Ince. Hearst reportedly believed that Chaplin was having an affair with his girlfriend, Davies, and thinking that he was shooting Chaplin—he shot Ince instead. Many in Hollywood believe that Hearst built the Chateau for the widow of Ince as a gesture of atonement for her husband's death. From 1951 to 1973, the Chateau was a retirement home called the Fifield Manor. In recent years, it has been owned by a religious organization. 5930 Franklin.

44. Judy Garlands's First Home in Hollywood. On their first visit to Hollywood in 1926, four-year-old Judy and her family lived here in the Iris Hotel (the St Moritz in recent years). 5849 Sunset.

45. First Talking Picture. It was here in the Warner Brothers Studio in 1927 that Al Jolson made the first talking picture, *The Jazz Singer*. Built in 1919, the administrative building resembles a colonnaded, colonial mansion. In 1939, the building was converted into the 52 lane Sunset Bowling Center. Gene Autry purchased the studio from Paramount Studios and owned it for 18 years. It is now TV station Channel 5. 5858 Sunset.

CENTRAL HOLLYWOOD

Clint Eastwood does not have a star but James Nederlander? does.

Walk of Fame. In 1958, Hollywood decided to pay tribute to the artists who helped make Hollywood the most famous city in the world. This was accomplished by installing a sidewalk made up of coral terrazzo stars outlined in brass. Inside each star was to be the name of an honoree, also in brass. They called it the "The Walk of Fame."

In 1960, the first eight stars were installed at the northwest corner of Hollywood Boulevard and Highland Avenue. The first to have their name enshrined were film personalities Olive Borden, Ronald Coleman, Louise Fazenda, Preston Foster, Burt Lancaster, Edward Sedgwick, Ernest Torrence and Joanne Woodward.

Over 1900 other notables have been added to the original eight. Although most of the 1900 earned the right to their star, there are others whose qualifications are questionable. Some stars on the sidewalk contain the names of complete unknowns. In 1986, the "secret" selection committee of the Hollywood Chamber of Commerce embarrassed itself and Hollywood, when it seriously considered giving a star to an ape—the 1986 version of *King Kong*.

Honorees Must Pay $4800 for Their Star

Created to honor talented artists of the movie and TV industry, the Walk of Fame (or Walk of Shame, as some call it) has deteriorated into a shameful publicity tool for the Chamber of Commerce. Requirements to qualify are to fork over $4800 to the Chamber of Commerce, pose with Johnny Grant, and guarantee to draw a crowd.

Richard Burton, Peter Sellers, Lee Marvin, George Gershwin, Robert Redford, Clint Eastwood, Irving Berlin, Howard Hughes, George C. Scott, Dead End Kids, Sydney Greenstreet, and from the *Wizard of Oz,* Margaret Hamilton (witch) Bert Lahr (lion), and L. Frank Baum (author) are among those who do not have a star, but Pee Wee Herman, and a little-known disk jockey named Johnny Grant do. Grant, who gave himself the title of "honorary mayor" of Hollywood, heads the "secret" selection committee—the group that decides who gets a star and who doesn't.

CENTRAL HOLLYWOOD

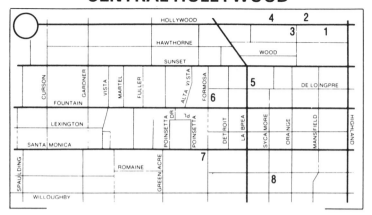

1.   Paramount Theater. Built in 1926 as a legitimate theatre and originally called the El Capitan. In 1942, it was converted into a movie theatre and renamed the Paramount. Disney Studios restored the inside of the theatre in 1991. 6838 Hollywood.

2.   Grauman's Chinese. More than two million people a year visit the forecourt of Hollywood's most famous theatre to view the concrete hand and foot prints of almost 180 celebrities. The first prints in concrete were those of actress Norma Talmadge on May 18, 1927. Grauman's opened in 1927 with the premiere of Cecil B. DeMille's silent film *The King of Kings*. 6925 Hollywood Blvd.

3.   Hollywood Roosevelt Hotel. Built in 1927, the Roosevelt has recently been refurbished. 7000 Hollywood Blvd.

4.   Hot Fudge Sundae Invented. It was here at C.C. Brown's Ice Cream Shop that the hot fudge sundae was invented. 7007 Hollywood.

5.   Chaplin Movie Studios. Built by Chaplin in 1918, the studio has been known as Herb Alpert's A&M Records since 1966. Former owners were Red Skelton and CBS. Chaplin's footprints are imbedded in concrete in front of stage 3. 1416 N. La Brea.

6.   French Village Movie set. Hidden behind the trees here is one of Hollywood's most unique apartment courts. The unusual shaped bungalows that resemble a small French village complete with a narrow cobblestone street, were built about 1920 by Charlie Chaplin for use as a movie set in one of his pictures. 1330 Formosa.

7.   Goldwyn Studios. Built in 1920 as the Hampton Studios, and purchased by Mary Pickford and Douglas Fairbanks Sr. in 1922, they named it the Pickford-Fairbanks Studios. Sam Goldwyn became partners with Pickford and Fairbanks in 1927 and renamed it the Goldwyn Studios. Goldwyn became sole owner in 1949. It has been the Warner Hollywood Studios in recent years. 1041 Formosa.

8.   Headquarters of Howard Hughes. In 1927, Hughes moved into this building with his Caddo Pictures, and turned it into a virtual "fortress" from where he ruled his empire. 7010 Romaine.

CENTRAL HOLLYWOOD

1. Hollywood Canteen. Founded by Bette Davis and John Garfield in 1942, the Canteen entertained servicemen during World War II. A four-story parking building is now on the site. 1451 Cahuenga.

2. Hollywood Ranch Market. Once famous as the market where the stars shopped. Replaced by a mini-mall in 1982. 1248 Vine.

3. Columbia Studios. Founded by Harry Cohn in 1921, the studio is located in what was once known as "poverty row" an area inhabited by small studios working on a shoestring. This was the home studio of Kim Novak, and The Three Stooges. 1438 Gower.

4. Silent Screen Star Dies of Alcoholism. Marie Prevost, an early Mack Sennett bathing beauty and a leading star in the 1920s, died of alcoholism here in her apartment in 1937. Living in near poverty, Prevost, who had been dead for several days, was found with her pet dachshund whining at her bedside. The dog had chewed up her arms and legs in a futile attempt to awaken her. Several empty whiskey bottles were found nearby. She was 38 years old. 6230 Afton Place.

5. Hollywood Studio Club. Opened in 1926, the club has served as the home for many young starlets, such as, Kim Novak, Gale Storm, Donna Reed, Janet Blair, Sharon Tate and Sally Struthers. Marilyn Monroe lived in room 334 in 1948. It is now the YWCA. 1215 Lodi.

6. Founder of South Hollywood. In 1893, Senator Cornelius Cole founded Colgrove (now South Hollywood). Cole died here in his home in the early 1920s. 6121 Lexington. In 1914, Cecil B. DeMille lived across the street at 6136 Lexington.

7. Actor Dies of Overdose. Phillip Van Zandt, 53, a character actor who appeared in over 300 films, died here in his apartment in 1958 of an overdose of sleeping pills. His last appearance was in the 1957 film *The Lonely Man.* 1225 Gower.

8. Mickey Rooney's First Pictures. It was here in 1926 that six-year-old Mickey Rooney (then known as Mickey McGuire) made many comedy film shorts. Known as Berwilla Studios in the early 1930s, Darmour studios in the late 1920s, and Majestic Pictures from 1932-35. The 1933 film *The Vampire Bat* starring Fay Wray and Melvyn Douglas was filmed here. 5823 Santa Monica.

CENTRAL HOLLYWOOD

1.   Jean Harlow Debut's in "Hells' Angel's." Built in 1919 as the Jasper Studio, it was here in 1927 that Howard Hughes made the silent movie *Hell's Angel's* in which a young Jean Harlow made her film debut. It was the Metropolitan Studio during the 1920s, and the Educational Studios in the early 1930s. It became the General Service Studios in 1934, and Francis Coppola's Zoetrope in 1980. It was here on stage 2 where Shirley Temple made her film debut, and the first *I Love Lucy* shows were made. In recent years it has been the Hollywood Center Studios. 1040 Las Palmas.

2.   Technicolor Film Lab. The famous color lab was located here for many years. 6311 Romaine.

3.   Hollywood's Phantom Studio. When the Metro Studios were built here in the late teens, it covered five city blocks, and was the second largest producer of films in Hollywood. It was here in 1921 that Rudolph Valentino made the film that made him famous, *The Four Horsemen of the Apocalypse*. In 1924, when Metro merged with Goldwyn Studios and became known as Metro-Goldwyn-Mayer, this site was abandoned, sold, and soon afterward destroyed. The old studio was quickly forgotten and vanished without a trace. Part of the site is now a huge parking lot. 6300 Romaine.

4.   Charlie Chaplin's First Studio. During 1916-17, Chaplin made the films *The Immigrant, The Floorwalker,* and *Easy Street* here at the Lone Star Studios. Buster Keaton made many of his comedy films here in the 1920s. The site is now a parking lot. 1025 Lillian Way.

5.   Make Room for Daddy. In the early 1920s, this site was an outdoor set on the backlot of the Metro studios. In the 1940s, new facilities were built and became known as the Motion Picture Studios. In the 1960s it was the Cinema General Studios. In recent years it has been the Television Center and Ren-Mar Studios. Danny Thomas filmed his TV show *Make Room for Daddy* here. 846 Cahuenga.

6.   Orphanage Where Marilyn Monroe Once Lived. The Los Angeles Orphan's Home was home for 10-year-old Marilyn during 1936-37. At night, from her second floor room, she would look out at the bright RKO Studio sign a few blocks away, and dream that some day she would become a famous movie star. The old building was destroyed in 1977 and a new one was built on the site. 815 El Centro.

CENTRAL HOLLYWOOD

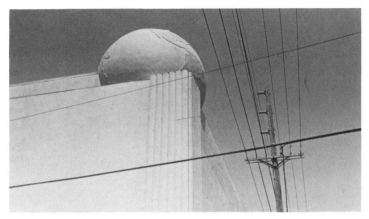

World globe of old RKO sign on top of sound stage.

7.   RKO Studios. Built in 1920-21 on what was once a part of the Hollywood Cemetery, this lot was first called the Robertson-Cole Studios. In 1923 it was the FBO Studios owned by Joseph Kennedy, father of President Kennedy. It became the RKO Studios in 1928, and Howard Hughes bought it in 1948. In 1957, Lucille Ball and Desi Arnaz bought the studio from Hughes. RKO is now part of Paramount Studio. Fred Astaire, Ginger Rogers and Gary Cooper made their films here. 780 N. Gower.

8.   Nickodell's. A favorite of the stars from Paramount and RKO Studios in the 1940s and 50s. 5507 Melrose.

9.   Marilyn Monroe Poses for Nude Calendar. Marilyn was paid $50 in May, 1949 to pose nude for her famous calendar here in the studio of photographer, Tom Kelley. 736 N. Seward.

10.   Ronald Reagan's Death Valley Days. Known as the Clune Studios in the 1920s and the California Studios in the 30s, where the "Hopalong Cassidy" westerns were made. It was here in the early 1960s at the Producers Studio, that Ronald Reagan made the *Death Valley Days* TV series. Rawleigh Studios in 1992. 650 N. Bronson.

11.   Hollywood's Oldest Studio. Built in 1917-18 as the Peralta Studios, and known today as Paramount Studios. It was the Brunton Studios in 1920, and the United Studios from 1921 to 1926. Many people claim that Rudolph Valentino made his films here. Valentino died before Paramount moved here in 1926. He made his Paramount pictures at the old Lasky Studio on Sunset and Vine. Even though Valentino probably never set foot on this lot, the city, in the 1970s named a street near the studio, Valentino Place. Clara Bow, Mae West, Bing Crosby and Bob Hope made films here. 5451 Marathon.

12.   Rudolph Valentino's Final Resting Place, Established in 1899, the Hollywood Cemetery is the burial place of many famous stars, and Hollywood pioneers. 6000 Santa Monica.

CENTRAL HOLLYWOOD

HOLLYWOOD MEMORIAL CEMETERY

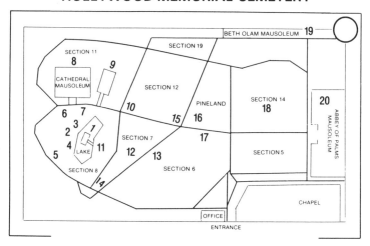

1. Copper and Railroad Magnate. The huge mausoleum on the lake island was built in 1920 at a cost of $250,000 by copper magnate and railroad owner, William A. Clark Jr. Clark, who founded the Los Angeles Philharmonic Symphony Orchestra in 1924, is entombed inside between his two wives and some of his art collection.

2. Marion Davies. Former girl friend of William Randolph Hearst, Davies' large white mausoleum with the name Douras, is a few feet from the Tyrone Power grave. She died of cancer in 1961 at age 64. Also in the tomb is her son-in-law, actor, Arthur Lake, (Dagwood Bumstead). Hearst, who died in 1951, is buried near San Francisco.

3. Tyrone Power. Located near the edge of the lake, the Power monument is bench-like with a large marble book standing at one end. Power died of a heart attack in 1958. He was 44.

Tyrone Power's lakeside grave. Hollwood can be seen in background.

CENTRAL HOLLYWOOD

HOLLYWOOD MEMORIAL CEMETERY
SECTION 8 OUTSIDE

4.   Actress Dies in "Fatty" Arbuckle Rape. While attending a wild party at a San Francisco hotel in 1921, bit actress, Virginia Rappe was the unfortunate victim of Hollywood's first and most famous scandal. Comedian Roscoe "Fatty" Arbuckle was accused of killing Rappe in a drunken and crude attempt to have sex with her. There have been many versions as to how Arbuckle had violated her. Officially, Miss Rappe, 26, died of a ruptured bladder. Arbuckle, tho acquitted, was banned from the movies, and died a broken man.

Rappe's Lover. Buried next to Miss Rappe is producer/director Henry "Pathe" Lehrman. In love with Rappe, he was planning to ask her to marry him. Crushed by her death, he buried her here, vowing that he would kill the "monster" Arbuckle if he ever met him again. Heartbroken, he faithfully visited her grave each week until his own death in 1946. His last request was that he be laid to rest next to his sweetheart, who he had never stopped loving. They lie side by side under simple headstones in the first row next to the lake.

5.   Cecil B. DeMille. Pioneer producer DeMille and his wife Constance are interred in twin crypts near the road. He died of a heart seizure in 1959 at age 77.

6.   Nelson Eddy. An opera singer, Eddy starred in several films with Jeanette MacDonald. He died of a stroke in 1967 at age 66.

7.   Studio Czar Harry Cohn. Cohn died of a heart attack in 1958 at age 58. Just months before his death, Cohn selected his final resting place here only six blocks from his beloved Columbia Studios. "I picked out a great plot" he told a friend. "It's right by the water, and I can see the studio from here." His twin marble monument is across the road from the Cathedral Mausoleum entrance.

8.   Hollywood Cathedral Mausoleum. See page 23.

9.   Douglas Fairbanks Sr. The large monument at the far end of the sunken gardens is one of Hollywood's most impressive star graves. A star in silent films, Fairbanks' coffin is encased in the sarcophagus that lies between the marble columns. Fairbanks, who was once married to Mary Pickford, died of a heart attack in 1939. He was 56. Pickford, who died in 1979, is buried in Forest Lawn, Glendale.

10.   Broadway Stores Founder. Arthur Letts.

11.   Adolph Menjou. Known as the best dressed man in Hollywood, Menjou died of hepatitis in 1963 at age 73.

12.   John T. Gower Hollywood Pioneer. Gower, a rancher, came to Hollywood in 1869. Gower Street is named in his honor.

13.   Senator Cornelius Cole Hollywood Pioneer. In 1893, Cole founded the town of Colegrove, now known as South Hollywood. Ten Hollywood streets are named after the Cole family.

CENTRAL HOLLYWOOD

HOLLYWOOD MEMORIAL CEMETERY
SECTION 8 OUTSIDE

14.   L. A's Most Unpopular Man. In 1896, Colonel Griffith J. Griffith donated over 3000 acres of land to Los Angeles, they named it Griffith Park. In 1903, Griffith, a heavy drinker and one of the most unpopular men in Los Angeles, was convicted of attempting to kill his wife. He shot her in the eye after accusing her of conspiring with the Pope to poison him and to overthrow the government. Found guilty, he was sentenced to two years in San Quentin. In 1930, the city reluctantly accepted a grant from his estate to build the Greek Theatre. Griffith died of liver trouble in 1919 at age 69. Only a handful of people attended his burial here. Tall obelisk at corner.

15.   Founder of Los Angeles Times. Harrison Gray Otis who died in 1917, founded the Times in 1881. Next to his tall obelisk monument is the monument of his daughter Marion Otis and his son-in-law, Harry Chandler. Next to the Chandler plot stands the huge memorial Otis erected for the twenty employees who were killed in a bomb blast that destroyed the Times building in 1910.

16.   Rocket Ship Headstone. The monument of pioneer graphic artist, Carl Bigsby, is an exact replica of the first Pioneer Atlas rocket. It reads: "Retired by God" and "Too bad . . . we had fun."

"Our Gang's" dog "Pete" on headstone of Carl "Alfalfa" Switzer.

17.   Our Gang's "Alfalfa." Carl Switzer, the freckle-faced member of "Our Gang" is buried in the second row from the curb. Switzer was shot and killed in 1959 in an argument over a $50 debt. He was 33.

18.   Mel Blanc. The "Man of a thousand voices" died in 1989 at age 81. His headstone near the curb reads "That's all Folks."

19.   Gangster Benjamin "Bugsy" Siegel. The former mobster, who was shot and killed in 1947, is buried in the Beth Olam Mausoleum. Entrance nearest to Gower St. Turn right at second aisle. His crypt is on the left near middle of section 2, third row from bottom.

20.   Abbey of Palms Mausoleum. See page 25.

CENTRAL HOLLYWOOD

HOLLYWOOD MEMORIAL CEMETERY

CATHEDRAL MAUSOLEUM SECTION 11

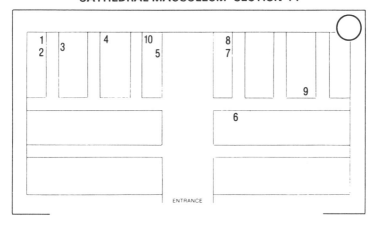

1.   Rudolph Valentino. When Rudolph Valentino died in 1926, several women committed suicide and a whole nation mourned him. A crowd of 10,000 jammed the cemetery here on the day that he was laid to rest in a magnificent silverbronze coffin, wearing a slave bracelet given to him by his last wife, actress Natacha Rambova. Until a more impressive mausoleum could be built for the famous star, he was placed temporarily in a vault that belonged to his friend and discoverer, writer June Mathis. Unfortunately, the grand plans for the huge monument were abandoned and Valentino to this day still rests in the borrowed wall crypt #1205. Ironically, Valentino, while alive, had stood here many times to place flowers on the crypt of Miss Mathis' mother, Virginia Mathis, who lies just below Valentino. The "Lady in Black" still attracts attention of the news media despite the fact the event was a publicity stunt begun in 1931. Rudolph Valentino died in New York of peritonitis on August 23rd, 1926. He was 31.

Rudolph Valentino's crypt in Hollywood Cemetery.

CENTRAL HOLLYWOOD

HOLLYWOOD MEMORIAL CEMETERY

CATHEDRAL MAUSOLEUM SECTION 11

2. The Woman Who Discovered Valentino. Writer June Mathis Balboni spotted unknown Rudolph Valentino at the Metro Studios in 1920, and insisted that the studio cast him in the lead of *The Four Horsemen of the Apocalypse*—the picture made Valentino a star. The first woman executive in the movie industry and Valentino's best friend, Miss Mathis died in 1927. Her crypt is to the left of Valentino.

3. Oscar Winner Peter Finch. For almost two years, Peter Finch was buried in an unmarked grave near the Marion Davies tomb until his widow moved him here in 1979. Finch, who died of a heart attack in 1977 at age 60, won an oscar for Best Actor in the 1976 film *Network.*

4. The Girl Who Was "Too Beautiful." Silent screen star Barbara LaMarr's movie career in Hollywood lasted only three years, but that brief

period of stardom earned her a place in Hollywood history as the most beautiful woman who ever appeared before a movie camera— she was known as "The Girl Who was Too Beautiful." Director Paul Bern once attempted suicide when she refused to marry him. (Bern later killed himself while married to Jean Harlow). Miss LaMarr's star faded when heavy drinking and "fast living" caused a nervous breakdown. In 1926, at age 30, she died in Altadena from what the doctors called overdieting. Her funeral

Barbara LaMarr

services at the mortuary (now a parking lot on Highland Avenue just north of Hollywood Boulevard) caused a riot.

5. Star Tap Dancer. Eleanor Powell was once called "The World's Greatest Female Tap Dancer," She died of cancer in 1982 at age 69. Her ashes are in the left wall of the main hallway.

6. Hollywood's Greatest Unsolved Murder. Director William Desmond Taylor's murder in 1922, (see page 68) ruined the careers of two actresses. His wall crypt bears the name, William Deane Tanner.

7. The Man Who Founded Hollywood. H. H. Wilcox founded Hollywood in 1887, (see page 10). Wilcox died in 1891.

8. The "Mother" of Hollywood. Daeida Wilcox Beveridge gave Hollywood it's name. (see page 8). She died of cancer in 1914.

9. Movie "Bad Guy." Peter Lorre co-starred in the *Maltese Falcon* and *Casablanca*. Lorre died of a stroke in 1964 at age 60. His ashes are in the bottom row of the Alcove of Reverance.

10. Rear View Mirror Inventor. Elmer Berger, the inventor of the auto rear view mirror died in 1952. Crypt 1405.

CENTRAL HOLLYWOOD

HOLLYWOOD MEMORIAL CEMETERY

ABBEY OF PALMS MAUSOLEUM

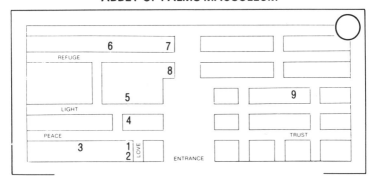

1. Talmadge Sisters. A super star during the silent era, Norma Talmadge, was once married to producer Joseph Schenck and George Jessel. She died of a cerebral stroke and pneumonia in 1957 at age 63. Constance, also an actress in silent films, died of pneumonia in 1973, at age 73. Sanctuary of Eternal Love.

2. Cecil Barbee. Former president of Coca-Cola Co. Just to the left of the door of the Talmadge crypt, near the bottom. Crypt 2403.

3. Clifton Webb. A popular character actor, Webb was nominated for academy awards in *Laura, The Razor's Edge* and *Sitting Pretty*. He died of a heart attack in 1966 at age 73. His crypt is in the Sanctuary of Peace. His mother Maybelle lies next to him. There are reports that Webb haunts the mausoleum hallway where he is entombed.

4. Jesse Lasky. In 1913, pioneer producer Jesse Lasky and Cecil B. DeMille produced the first full length movie made in Hollywood. Lasky was president of Famous Players-Lasky Studio which later became Paramount Pictures. He died in 1958 at age 78. Crypt 2196.

5. Darla Hood. A member of the "Our Gang" Comedy, Darla died in 1979 at age 48. Her close friend, Carl "Alfalfa" Switzer is buried outside the mausoleum (see page 22).

6. Victor Fleming. A director at MGM for many years, Fleming directed the films *The Wizard of Oz* and *Gone with the Wind.* He died in 1949 at age 66. Crypt #2081.

7. Renee Adoree. A silent screen star and former French circus performer, Miss Adoree appeared in the 1925 film *The Big Parade.* She died of tuberculosis in 1933 at age 34. Crypt #319.

8. Louis Calhern. A distinguished character actor in the 1930s and 40s. He died of a heart attack in 1956 at 61. His ashes are just inside the mausoleum entrance, on the left.

9. Joan Hackett. Actress died of cancer at age 49 in 1983. Her crypt reads: "Go away, I'm asleep." 11th crypt from outside door.

WILSHIRE DISTRICT

1. Mae West's Penthouse Home. When Mae West arrived in Hollywood in 1932 she moved into the Ravenswood Apartments here. When she died at age 87 in 1980, she still occupied the same apartment. Her home of over 48 years was finished in a white-on-white decor with gilt-on-white furniture. 570 No. Rossmore.

2. Singer Russ Columbo Killed. Columbo was shot and killed here in 1934. While he and a friend were inspecting an antique gun, it went off and struck him above the eye. Columbo and Carole Lombard planned to marry at the time. 584 Lillian Way.

Hollywood home used in television's "Happy Days."

3. "Happy Days" House. The Cunninghams home seen in the TV series *Happy Days* is located here. 565 N. Cahuenga.

4. Home of Nat "King" Cole. When Cole bought this home in 1948, nearby home owners joined in an effort to keep the black singer out. After Cole went door-to-door introducing himself to neighbors, ojections were dropped. Cole died here in 1965. 401 S. Muirfield.

5. Home of Muhammad Ali. Fremont Place is one of Los Angeles' most exclusive private streets. The mansion of former World Heavyweight Champion Muhammad Ali is at 55 Fremont Place.

6. **Norma Desmond's "Sunset Boulevard" Mansion.** The estate used in the 1950 film *Sunset Boulevard* as the home of Norma Desmond, was built here in 1922 by William O. Jenkins. At the time of the filming, it was the residence of Mrs. J. Paul Getty. The mansion was torn down in 1957. 641 Irving. N.W. corner of Wilshire.

7. **Home of Mayor Tom Bradley.** The Getty house, once the home of George F. Getty, has been the residence of Mayor Tom Bradley during his years as mayor. 605 S. Irving.

8. **Robert Kennedy Assassinated.** Sirhan Sirhan shot and killed Robert F. Kennedy here in the Ambassador Hotel in 1968. The famous Cocoanut Grove was located here. Boarded up in 1988, the hotel was awaiting demolition in 1993. 3400 Wilshire Blvd.

The original "Hat" Brown Derby as it looked in 1984.

9. **The "Hat"ᵘ Brown Derby Restaurant.** Built in 1926 as a coffee shop by the husband of actress Gloria Swanson, the remodeled Derby is now part of a mini-shopping mall. 3377 Wilshire Blvd.

10. **Home of Actress Mabel Normand.** When director William Desmond Taylor was murdered in 1922, his girlfriend, Mabel Normand lived here. The site is now a parking lot. 3089 Seventh.

11. **40-Room Mansion of Mary Miles Minter.** Actress and girlfriend of director William Desmond Taylor at the time of his murder in 1922, Minter owned "Casa de Marguerite," the 40-room mansion that is now home for unwed mothers. 701 S. New Hampshire.

12. **The "Real McCoy" Murders His Girlfriend.** In 1924, Norman Selby, better known as "Kid" McCoy, murdered his girlfriend here in her apartment #212. McCoy, was once the Welter and Middle-weight Champion of the World. His name evoked the famous expression "The Real McCoy." Paroled in 1932, broke and alone, McCoy killed himself in 1940 by taking poison. 2819 Leeward.

EAST HOLLYWOOD

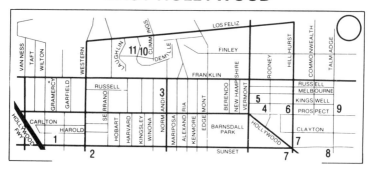

1. Dracula's Last Home. Famous for his film portrayal of "Count Dracula," Bela Lugosi died broke and forgotten here in his small apartment in 1956. Just one year before his death, Lugosi had been released from a state hospital where he had been committed for treatment as a drug addict. 5620 Harold Way.

2. John Wayne Makes Film Debut. In 1917, William Fox built Fox Studios here on both sides of Western Ave. It was here that Tom Mix, Buck Jones and Theda Bara made films. John Wayne made his first film here in 1928. In 1935, Fox merged with Twentieth Century Pictures, and later moved to studios near Beverly Hills. The old lot was destroyed in the 1960s. 1400-1500 N. Western.

3. Hollywood's Most Bizarre Suicide. Hollywood is still puzzled by the bizarre suicide of actor Albert Dekker. Although he made almost 100 films, Dekker is remembered mainly for his role of the sinister "Dr. Cyclops," a mad scientist who shrunk humans down to doll size. In 1968, Dekker killed himself in an original style never duplicated by any other Hollywood star. He was found in the bath-

Albert Dekker

room of his apartment here—hanging by his neck at the end of a rope that was tied to the shower curtain rod. The rope, knotted tightly around his neck, was also wrapped around both of his legs and around one of his arms. His hands were bound with a pair of handcuffs, and two hyperdermic needles were stuck in his body. Police originally listed his strange death as a suicide. Several days later, the coroner reported his death was an "accident," saying "We have no information that Mr. Dekker planned to take his own life." Dekker left a bizarre trail of death behind him—over 20 actors and actresses who had appeared in movies with him, died tragic deaths, either by suicide, murder or unusual circumstances. His only son committed suicide in 1957, and his girlfriend's daughter killed herself. In 1944, Dekker served as a California State Assemblyman representing Hollywood. 1731 N. Normandie.

EAST HOLLYWOOD

4. Tree Cross From Hiroshima A-Bomb Blast. A cross carved from the charred wood of a tree felled by the atomic bomb that was dropped on Hiroshima, Japan in 1945, stands near the altar of The Mt. Hollywood Church here. The cross was presented to the church in the late 1940s by a group of survivors who were badly burned in the 1945 Hiroshima blast. 4607 Prospect Avenue.

Store front on right was Walt Disney's first studio in 1925.

5. Birth Place of Mickey Mouse? Walt Disney and his brother Roy opened their first studio here in 1925. It was in this tiny store that Walt and his friend, animator Ub Iwerks, began to experiment with their many cartoon characters, one of which eventually became known as Mickey Mouse. Iwerks is said to have been the creator of Mickey Mouse, not Walt. 4649 Kingswell.

6. Walt Disney's First Home in Hollywood. When Walt Disney came to Hollywood in 1923, he moved into this house with his uncle, Robert Disney. Walt paid $5 a week for room and board. It was in a small garage in back of the house that Walt built his first cartoon stand with which he made his first Hollywood cartoon film, *Alice's Wonderland.* When Roy Disney was married in the living room here in 1925, Walt served as best man. The little garage that Walt used as a workshop, sat forgotten and neglected until 1978 when its existence was brought to light by the author. In 1981, the old garage was sold and removed from the property. 4406 Kingswell.

7. Hollywood's Largest Movie Set. In 1916, D.W. Griffith made his classic silent film *Intolerance* here on this site. The enormous "Babylon" set, built for use in the film, was the largest outdoor movie set ever built in Hollywood. In 1915, the lot was known as Majestic Reliance Studios. It was the Fine Arts Studio in the 1920s and the Talisman Studios in the 30s. The set was on the NE corner of Sunset and Hillhurst, the studio was on the SW corner. 4400-4500 Sunset.

8.   East Side Kids Studio. Called the Monogram Studios From 1940 to 1950, it was here that "The East Side Kids" (Bowery Boys) and the Charlie Chan series were filmed. Built in 1912 by Sigmund "Pop" Lubin, other owners included: Kalem, 1913, Willis & Ingles, 1917, Jesse Hampton, 1918, Charles Ray, 1920, Allied Artists, 1952, and Colorvision TV in 1967. KCET-TV Channel 28, bought the studio in 1970. Only a few old buildings remain today. 4376 Sunset Drive.

9.   Vitagraph Movie Studios. One of the largest studios in Hollywood, Vitagraph was built in 1917-18 by Albert Smith and J. Stuart Blackton. Actress Norma Talmadge made many of her pictures here.In 1925, the Warner brothers, bought it and renamed it Warner Brothers-Vitagraph Studios. In 1948, ABC bought the site. It is now the home of KABC-TV Channel 7. 4151 Prospect.

10.   Mansion of Cecil B. DeMille. When DeMille bought this home in 1916, comedian Charlie Chaplin lived next door. In I920, Demille bought the Chaplin house and connected the two homes. When he made the film *King of Kings* in 1926, he reproduced the huge Garden of Gethsemane set in the olive grove in back of the estate where he filmed scenes for the movie. After DeMille died in 1959, the mansion was kept exactly as it was while he was alive until it was sold in 1988. In 1989, it sold again for over $5 million. 2010 DeMille

11.   W.C. Fields/Lily Tomlin Home. Directly across the street from the DeMille mansion was the home of W.C. Fields and his young companion, Carlotta Monti from 1940 to 1946. Fields died in 1946. In 1942, Anthony Quinn's 2-year-old son (DeMille's grandson) drowned in a small pond on Field's front lawn. The Spanish villa was panelled throughout with rich oak and walnut, but when actress Lily Tomlin bought the home in 1980, she painted over the beautiful rich woods with flat wall pink paint. 2015 DeMille Drive.

W.C. Fields' last home in the Hollywood Hills.

HOLLYWOOD HILLS

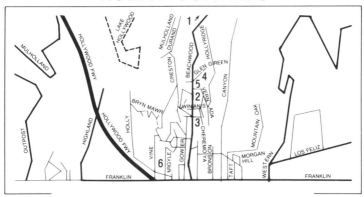

1. The Hollywood Sign.

Hollywood's famous sign was built in 1923 as an ad for a real estate development. Its 50-foot high letters originally read HOLLWOODLAND until 1949 when the city tore down the last four letters. Located on Mt. Lee (part of the old Sherman and Clark ranch), the sign had 5000 electric lights that flashed on and off nightly.

2. Actress Leaps to Her Death from the Hollywood Sign.

Actress Lillian Millicent (Peg) Entwistle was born in England to parents who were both stage performers. It was predestined that Peg would grow up with the burning desire to become a successful actress. In 1925, she made her debut on Broadway in the play *Hamlet.* In 1927, at age 19, she became one of the youngest actresses to ever star in a hit play on Broadway. After a successful string of performances, her luck began to change—her 1931-32 Broadway season was disastrous. In April of 1932, she moved to Hollywood hoping to find new success in the movies. After several months of looking for work, she was signed to a contract by RKO Studios. In her first picture *Thirteen Women,* she had only a small bit part. When the film was completed. the studio declined to pick up her option—her spirits were crushed. On the evening of September 18, 1932, the depressed actress left her home here where she lived with her

Peg Entwistle

uncle, and walked up to the end of Beachwood Drive. She then climbed laboriously up through the dense brush of the rough terrain toward the huge thirteen-letter sign at the top of the hill. After reaching the base of the sign, she climbed up the ladder to the top of the 50-foot letter "H." No one will ever know how long the despondent, but determined young actress stood on top of the sign that overlooked the town that had rejected her. Finally, with the sign's thousands of lights flashing on and off—Peg dove to her death into the darkness below. She was 24 years old. Miss Entwistle is the only known person to commit suicide by jumping off the sign. 2428 Beachwood.

HOLLYWOOD HILLS

House where Paul Kelly beat love rival to death.

3.   Hollywood's Almost Perfect Murder. Actor Paul Kelly was one of Hollywood's busiest actors. In his 30-year movie career, he appeared in over 400 films, in many of which he played the role of a "tough guy." But no role was as important as the "for real" part he played when he "almost got away with murder." In 1927, Kelly fell in love with actress Dorothy Mackaye, who at the time was married to stage actor, Ray Raymond. When Raymond discovered that Kelly was

Paul Kelly

his wife's lover, he invited Kelly to his home here to discuss a possible solution to the "love triangle." Their talk instead turned into a fist fight in which Raymond suffered a severe beating at the hands of the stronger Kelly. When Raymond died several days later, Kelly and Mrs. Raymond called in a physician with whom they made "a deal." After $500 exchanged hands, the doctor reported that Raymond had died of natural causes. Funeral services were quickly arranged, with cremation to follow. While services for the dead man were being conducted, the coroner, who was acting on an anonymous tip, halted the ceremony and ordered an autopsy that revealed Raymond expired from a brutal beating, Kelly was convicted of murder and Mrs. Raymond of conspiracy. They both served terms in San Quentin. Shortly after their release, Kelly married the widow of the man he had killed. 2261 Cheremoya.

4.   Actor Peter Duel Kills Self. Star of the TV series *Alias Smith and Jones* (as Joshua Smith), Duel shot himself here in his home in 1971. He was 31. 2552 Glen Green Terrace.

5. Hollywood's Greatest Lover Dies in Gas Oven. Larry Edmunds owned a bookshop in Hollywood in the 1930s from which he sold books and pornography from a suitcase to the writers in the studios. One of his customers, director Billy Wilder said Edmunds was a homosexual. Edmunds' business partner said Edmunds loved women and called him "Hollywood's greatest seducer." Edmunds, who also loved books and booze, had great charm and was a hypnotic conversationalist. He became friends with John Barrymore, W.C. Fields, Marlene Dietrich, and writer Thomas Wolfe. He never stalked women—they stalked him. Reportedly, he seduced 75 per cent of the secretaries in the studios. He did it in their apartments, on the beach, and in the Hollywood Hills. He did it with Dolores Del Rio, Margo, Ann Harding, Mary Astor, Margaret Sullivan, Paulette Goddard, Marlene Dietrich, Myrna Loy, Lupe Velez and others. In 1940, Edmunds began to drink heavily. He was in and out of drying out hospitals and sanitariums. One day in 1941, when Edmunds had not shown up at the book store for two days, his partner went to Edmunds' home here and found the 35-year-old Edmunds lying dead on the kitchen

Larry Edmunds

floor—he had stuck his head in the gas oven. A suicide note explained the holes gashed in the wall. He had made the holes with a knife, because he was chopping off the heads of the little men that were creeping out of the wall. He realized that he was a hopeless case, and decided to take his own life. Among his effects found in the small house were six diaphrams, each one with the name of a different woman. Two were famous actresses, a female screen-writer, two were wives of famous stars, and one the wife of a screenwriter. Also found were all the novels of his old friend, writer Thomas Wolfe, in which Wolfe had written personal expressions of his love for Edmunds in the books blank pages. 2470 N. Beachwood Canyon (small house in back)

6. World's Greatest Tennis Star Dies Broke and Disgraced. Big Bill Tilden dominated the tennis courts of the world in the 1920s. He won seven U.S. national championships, six in a row from 1920 through 1925. He won the Wimbledon title in 1920, 1921, and 1930, and played on the American Davis Cup team eleven years. He was the darling of the Hollywood movie crowd. Some still call him the greatest tennis player who ever lived. In the late 1940s Tilden was arrested and sentenced to two jail terms, one for committing homosexual acts with a 14-year-old boy, and one for violating his parole. Most of his friends turned their backs on him, and his name was stricken from the alumni files at Pennsylvania U. In June, 1953, alone, and living on handouts, Tilden, 60, died of a heart attack here in his apartment. Less than 100 turned out for his funeral. 2025 N. Argyle.

HOLLYWOOD HILLS

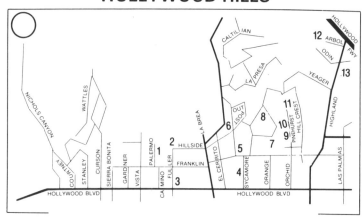

1. Ozzie Nelson Haunts Former Home. For over twenty-five years, Ozzie and Harriet Nelson lived in this home in Hollywood.

Located near Hollywood Blvd., it was here that Rick and David grew up. After Ozzie died in 1975, Harriet lived alone in the house until she sold it in 1980. Soon after the new owners moved in, they discovered that their famous home was quite unusual. Many strange and mysterious events began to happen, including doors that suddenly opened and closed—with nobody near them, lights and faucets that turned on and off—by themselves. The owners are convinced that the mischieveous incidents are the work of Ozzie Nelson's ghost. 1822 Camino Palermo.

Ozzie Nelson

Ghost of Ozzie Nelson playing tricks in Hollywood home?

HOLLYWOOD HILLS

Stairway is all that is left of former Huntington Hartford mansion.

2. Ruins of Huntington Hartford Estate. Just a few blocks north of Hollywood Blvd. lie the remains of a once beautiful 148 acre estate. After passing through the main gates leading into the grounds, a crumbling road takes you past the foundation and steps of what was once an English-Gothic mansion. Further up the curving road are the remains of tennis courts, two swimming pools and several cottages. Many exotic plants and trees grow out of control on the grounds. Called "The Pines," the estate was built in 1919-20 by Carman Randolph Runyon, who sold it to Irish tenor, John McCormack in the late 1920s. In 1942, supermarket magnate, Huntington Hartford purchased the estate. He owned it until the early 1960s, during which time he allowed it to deteriorate. Abandoned for over 30 years, the only structure intact on the grounds, is a small stone building, which McCormack once used as a studio to make his recordings. The property is one of the most serene in Hollywood. 2000 Fuller.

3. Cudahy Meat Packing Heir Kills Self. Louella Parsons called the home that once stood here, "the jinx mansion" after John P. Cudahy, son of the meat packing family committed suicide here by shooting off the top of his head in 1921. The mansion, built in 1904, was the home of such families as the Dunlops, Hersheys, and Ralphs. In the mid 1920s, the ill-fated home was purchased by producer Joseph Schenck and actress Norma Talmadge. In 1940, the home was torn down and a large apartment complex was built, and for the next 41 years, the Peyton Hall apartments were the home of countless movie stars. In 1981, it too, was destroyed. In 1986, a new apartment complex was built on the site. 7269 Hollywood Blvd.

4. Masquers Club. Founded in 1925, The Masquers Club was located here for over 60 years until the old clubhouse was destroyed in 1986 for a new development. 1765 Sycamore.

5. Janis Joplin Dies of Overdose. Rock singer Janis Joplin died of a heroin-morphine overdose here in a room of the former Landmark Hotel in 1970. While still alive, Joplin had set aside $2,500 for her own wake. The Grateful Dead provided the music for the 200 guests who had received invitations that read: "Drinks are on Pearl." She was 27 years old. .7047 Franklin Ave.

6. Hollywood's Most Historical Site. One of the most historical events in California history occurred here in an old adobe house in 1847 with the signing of the peace treaty that ended the U.S. Mexican War. The old abobe was the first home ever built in Hollywood. In the late 1800s, General Harrison Gray Otis, founder of The Los Angeles Times bought the property including the adobe. He named the old house "The Outpost," and lived in it until his death in 1917. In the mid 1920s, the adobe, which sat at the intersection of Outpost and Hillside was destroyed for a housing development. (The home of TV's Bob Barker is on the site, SW corner).   1900 Outpost Drive.

7. The Magic Castle. The beautiful three-story, 17-room victorian mansion here was built in 1909 by banker Rollin B. Lane. It has served as a private club for magicians in recent years. 7001 Franklin.

8. Authentic Oriental Palace. In 1914, the Bernheimer brothers purchased this 300-foot hill overlooking Hollywood and built a palace that was an exact replica of one of the most beautiful palaces in Japan. Hundreds of craftsmen were brought from the Orient to carve out each detail of the palace. Named the "Yamishiro," it is now a restaurant with a breathtaking view of L.A. 1999 Sycamore.

9. Home of "Tarzan" Author Edgar Rice Burroughs. Creator of "Tarzan," Burroughs lived in this home in 1934. It was here that he wrote the book *Tarzan and Jane.* 2029 Pinehurst.

10. Hollywood's First Art Director Commits Murder-Suicide. Wilford Bucklin came to Hollywood in 1913 to work with Cecil B. DeMille on the movie *The Squaw Man.* In 1946, Bucklin, 80, the originator of interior film lighting, killed his 36-year-old insane son, then committed suicide here. 2035 Pinehurst.

11. The Lady at the End of the Road. Carrie Jacobs-Bond is world famous as the composer of the songs, *I Love You Truly,* and *The End of a Perfect Day.* Her home here, which she named "The End of the Road," was a shrine to the art lovers of the world in the 1920s and 30s. Carrie built her beautiful home and gardens in 1917. The home still stands at the end of this street. 2042 Pinehurst.

12. The Hollywood Bowl. The first concerts and outdoor Easter sunrise services were held here in 1921. 2301 Highland.

13. Silent Screen Museum. After 50 years of use for storage at Paramount Studios, the former horse barn where Cecil B. DeMille and Jesse Lasky made their first Hollywood film *The Squaw Man* in 1913, is now the Hollywood Studio Museum. 2100 Highland.

HOLLYWOOD HILLS

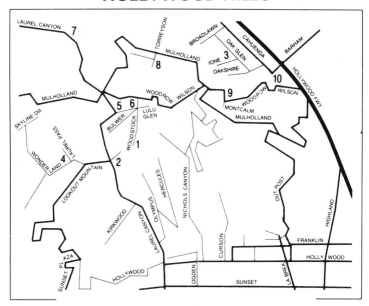

1. Two Church Officials Murdered on Canyon Estate. Two leaders of The Church of Naturalism were shot to death here on the church's six-acre Laurel Canyon estate in 1982. Police suspected that drugs were involved in the killings. 2500 Woodstock Road.

2. "Haunted" Ruins of Harry Houdini's Former Home. The weed covered stairway clinging to the steep hillside here leads to the ruins of the former 1920s estate of magician Harry Houdini. The only building still intact on the grounds are the servants quarters. Nearby canyon residents tell of strange happenings on the hilltop site. Some believe that the old estate is haunted by Houdini. 2398 Laurel Canyon.

Stairway leading to ruins of Harry Houdini's haunted estate.

HOLLYWOOD HILLS

Hollywood Hills home where John Matuszak died at age 38.

3. Football Star/Actor John Matuszak found dead. A star for the Oakland Raiders from 1976-81, the "Tooz" died here in his home in 1989 of a drug related heart attack. 3429 Oak Glen.

4. Five People Bludgeoned to Death. In 1981, five people were found beaten to death here. The sale of drugs were connected with the massacre. Porno star John Holmes was tried and acquitted of the murders in 1982. 8763 Wonderland Dr.

5. Actress Inger Stevens Dies from Drug Overdose. Miss Stevens, best known for her portrayal of a swedish housekeeper on the TV series *The Farmer's Daughter*, committed suicide here in 1970 by taking a drug overdose. She was 35 years old. Miss Stevens had attempted suicide once before in 1959 when her reported romance with Bing Crosby came to an end. 8000 Woodrow Wilson Dr.

6. Actress Gia Scala Dies of Drug-Alcohol Overdose. Miss Scala died here in 1972 of acute ethanol and barbiturate intoxication. She was 38. A few years earlier, she had tried to kill herself by jumping off of the Waterloo Bridge in London. 7944 Woodrow Wilson Dr.

7. Silent Screen Star Murdered on Halloween Night. Silent screen idol, Ramon Novarro was murdered here in his bedroom on Halloween night in 1968. He was brutally beaten to death by two young brothers he had "picked-up" on Hollywood Blvd. Police said he was killed after a violent struggle which left overturned furniture and splotches of blood in three rooms. Novarro, a Latin lover type in the 1920s, and a close friend of Rudolph Valentino, starred in the film *Ben Hur* in 1926. A lifelong bachelor, Novarro, 69, was troubled by drinking problems for many years. In 1980, a young actor who owned the secluded Spanish home, turned it into a shrine for the dead star. Many people who visited the house tell of an eerie feeling surrounding it, and some say that Novarro haunts the ill-fated home. A new home was built on the site in 1991. 3110 Laurel Canyon Blvd.

Errol Flynn's infamous Mulholland House.

8. Errol Flynn's "House of Pleasure. "Actor Errol Flynn designed and built his home here in 1942 at a cost of $125,000. He turned the home into a fortress of bacchanalian amusements, including installation of one-way mirrors in the ceilings of the bedrooms so that he and his friends could observe his famous houseguests making love. Flynn, Hollywood's best known rogue and casanova, once said of the home: "Strange people wended their way up the hill to the Mulholland house. Among them pimps, sports, bums, down at the heels actors, queers, athletes, sightseers, process servers, phonies, salesmen— everything in the world." And of course there were pretty girls—the more the merrier. Former owners were Richard Dreyfuss, and singers Stuart Hamblin and Rick Nelson. It was Nelson's last home. The house was torn down in June 1988. 3100 Torreyson Pl.

9. Actress Shoots Self in Suicide. A successful Broadway stage actress, Aleta Alexander had been in Hollywood only a few months before she shot and killed herself here in 1935 in the yard of the home where she lived with her husband of four months, film star Ross Alexander. Police reported that her death was the result of frustrated ambitions and an unsuccessful fight to obtain film roles. Henry Fonda, a close friend of the Alexanders, said that when Aleta discovered that her new husband was spending time with other women, she took his rifle and killed herself. She was 28 years old. Thirteen months later, Alexander, suffering from guilt feelings, killed himself with the same rifle (see page 82). 7357 Woodrow Wilson.

10. Actor Murdered in Drug Deal. "Bad guy" actor Frank Christi who appeared in the film *The Godfather*, and the television shows *Charlie's Angels*, and the *Rockford Files*, died screaming for mercy in a hail of bullets here in the carport of his home in 1982. Police believe that Christi, who was out of work, was probably gunned down by drug dealers. 6969 Woodrow Wilson Dr.

WEST HOLLYWOOD

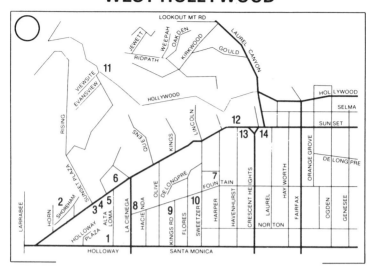

1. Sal Mineo Murdered Near Sunset Strip. On a February night in 1976, actor Sal Mineo was returning to his apartment here, when he was attacked and stabbed in the chest by a robber as he was getting out of his car in the carport behind the building where he lived. Neighbors found Mineo dead of a stab wound that had penetrated his heart. In his hand was a script of a play that he had been rehearsing, *P.S. Your Cat is Dead.* He was 37 years old. Mineo, a bisexual who had never married, appeared in the 1955 film, *Rebel Without a Cause,*

Sal Mineo

with James Dean, Natalie Wood and Nick Adams. All died a violent or unusual death. 8563 Holloway Drive.

2. Diane Linkletter Dies in Sixth Floor Death Leap. In 1969, Diane Linkletter, daughter of television star Art Linkletter, jumped to her death from her sixth floor apartment here. While talking to a friend about having experienced a bad LSD trip which caused hallucinations that made her fear that she was losing her sanity, she suddenly jumped out of the kitchen window. Her friend tried to stop her but could only catch the belt loops on her dress. 8787 Shoreham Dr.

3. Trocadero Restaurant. Opened in 1934 by W.R. Wilkerson, and closed in 1946. Only the three steps that led to its front door remain on the S.E. corner of Sunset Plaza. 8610 Sunset Blvd.

4. Mocambo Night Club. When the Mocambo opened in 1939, it became the favorite night spot of the stars before it closed in 1958. The site has been a parking lot for the Playboy offices. 8588 Sunset.

WEST HOLLYWOOD

Dino's Lodge used in TV's 77 Sunset Strip.

5.   Restaurant Used in TV's "77 Sunset Strip." From 1958 to 1964, Dino's Lodge, then owned by Dean Martin, was used as the location for the television show *77 Sunset Strip*. A landmark on the Strip, the restaurant was torn down in early 1989. 8524 Sunset.

6.   Ciro's, Hollywood's Grandest Night Club. Opened in 1939 by W. R. Wilkerson. From 1942 to 1957, when it closed, it was owned by Herman Hover. It is now The Comedy Store. 8433 Sunset Blvd.

7.   Marilyn Monroe Attempts Suicide. After her lover and benefactor, Johnny Hyde died in 1948, Monroe attempted suicide by taking an overdose of sleeping pills while living here with her drama coach, Natasha Lytess. 1309 N. Harper.

8.   Actress/Singer Dorothy Dandridge Dies of Overdose. In 1954, Dorothy Dandridge was the first black ever to be nominated for an Academy Award for acting in a major role in *Carmen Jones*. In 1965, she was broke and deeply in debt. A week before Thanksgiving of the same year, she was found dead here in her apartment—she had taken an overdose of a drug she had been taking for depression. She was 42. Her bank account contained only $2. 8495 Fountain Ave.

9.   Actor Jack Cassidy Dies in Penthouse Fire. Actor Jack Cassidy, father of Shaun Cassidy and former husband of Shirley Jones was burned to death in a fire here in his fourth floor apartment penthouse in 1976. He was 49. 1221 N. Kings Rd.

10.   Unsolved Murder of Actress Karen Kupcinet. On Thanksgiving Day in 1963, the nude body of Miss Kupcinet, 22, was found strangled here in her apartment. Still unsolved, detectives termed her murder "a riddle from day one." 1227 N. Sweetzer.

11.   Comedian Lenny Bruce Dies of Morphine Overdose. Known as the "foul-mouthed" comedian, Bruce, 41, died here in his home in 1966 after injecting himself with morphine. 8825 Hollywood.

WEST HOLLYWOOD

Bungalow where John Belushi died of an overdose.

12.   John Belushi Bows Out on Sunset Strip. The Chateau Marmont stands proudly at the head of the famous "Strip." For over 50 years, the exclusive residential hotel has been the favorite of many show business personalities such as Jean Harlow, Greta Garbo and

John Belushi

Errol Flynn. It was also the choice of comedian John Belushi. It was here on March 5, 1982 that Belushi, the star of TV's "Saturday Night Live" and the movie *Animal House,* was found dead in his bungalow from an overdose of cocaine and heroin. In an interview several months before he died, Belushi predicted his death when he declared, "I'm going to die young. I just can't stop destroying myself." "It was like he had a death wish," his friends said, "he was speeding along the fast lane—racing to his own funeral." On March 9, 1982, as snowflakes floated gently to the ground, Belushi, 33, was buried in a small cemetery in Martha's Vineyard. 8221 Sunset. Bungalow #2.

13.   Allah Nazimova's Garden of Allah. Opened in 1926, the Garden's bungalows and pool were the most popular in Hollywood. Torn down in 1959 for a bank, but a miniature model of the Garden can be seen inside the bank's lobby. 8152 Sunset.

14.   Schwabs the Drugstore of the Stars. It was here in 1939 that composer Harold Arlen wrote the song "Over the Rainbow." While passing the store one evening he used the light from its windows to write down the famous melody that had suddenly come to him. Lana Turner was NOT discovered here. Schwabs closed in 1985 and was torn down in 1989. 8024 Sunset Blvd.

FAIRFAX DISTRICT

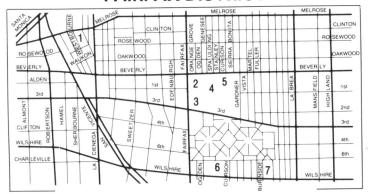

1.   World's First Movie Star Kills Self With Ant Paste. In the early 1900s when film players were not known by name, actress Florence Lawrence was known as "The Biograph Girl" and "The Imp Girl." When she was billed under her real name in 1910, she became the first player ever to be known to the public by name. She was also the first star to be part of a publicity stunt and first to be given a contract. In 1915, she suffered facial burns while filming a scene. Unable to get work because of scars, she was soon forgotten. In 1938, at age 52, she swallowed ant paste here in her home. 532 Westbourne.

2.   Gilmore Stadium Home of the Rams. It was here in 1947 that the Rams played their first game. Built in 1934, Gilmore Stadium was destroyed in 1952 to make room for CBS TV. 7800 Beverly.

3.   Oldest Home in Hollywood. Hidden by trees and shrubbery here in the middle of Farmers Market is one of Los Angeles' little known secrets, an adobe home over 140 years old. The home, built in 1852 was the birthplace in 1887 of oil producer, Earl Gilmore. It was on Gilmore's land that Farmers Market was started in 19?? Gilmore died in the adobe in 1964, in the bed he was born in. Today, his bedroom is kept exactly as it was at the time of his death. 300 N. Fairfax.

Oldest home in Hollywood sits unnoticed in Farmers Market.

4. Gilmore Field. Gilmore stood between where CBS is now and where the Pan Pacific Auditorium used to be. Built in the late 1930s, the site is now a small park. The Hollywood Stars played their last game here in 1957. 7750 Beverly Blvd.

5. Pan Pacific Auditorium. Built in 1935 and termed one of the most important examples of streamline moderne architecture in the country. The building was destroyed by fire in 1989. 7600 Beverly.

Pan Pacific Auditorium before its destruction by fire.

6. World's Richest Deposit of Ice Age Fossils. Since the La Brea Tarpits was formed over 40,000 years ago, almost two million fossils have been discovered here. 5801 Wilshire Blvd.

7. Movie Star Turned Hot-Dog Vendor Commits Suicide.
Actor/comedian Karl Dane was a big star during the silent era. He owned a mansion in the Hollywood Hills and was recognized wherever

he went. Then came talking pictures and his voice was unsuited for sound— his movie career was over. Embittered, he tried to rehabilitate himself as a carpenter and mechanic. He kept hoping for a "comeback" that never came. He suffered the final indignity, when he was forced to operate a small hot-dog stand outside the gates of MGM, the studio where just a few years before, he had been a star. He gave up all hopes in 1934, when he seated him-

Karl Dane

self in a chair in his apartment, spread his old clippings on the floor—then shot himself. He was 48. He lay unclaimed in the morgue until MGM buried him in Hollywood Cemetery. 626 S. Burnside.

BEVERLY HILLS

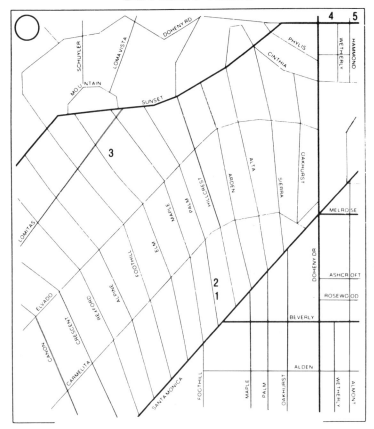

1.   Marilyn Monroe/Joe Dimaggio Honeymoon Home. After their wedding in 1954, the newlyweds spent their nine-month long marriage here. 508 N. Palm Dr.

2.   Last Home of Jean Harlow. Harlow was living here when she died of uremic poisoning in 1937. 512 N. Palm Dr.

3.   Video Executive and Wife Murdered. Millionaire, Jose Menendez, and his wife, Kitty, were murdered here in their home in August 1989. Killed by shotgun blasts to the head, he was shot five times and she ten. The couples' sons, Lyle, 22, and Eric, 19, were charged with murdering their parents. Former occupants of the home were singers, Elton John and Michael Jackson. 722 N. Elm.

4.   Gangster Mickey Cohen Shot in Gunfight. In 1948, Cohen was shot here at Sherry's Restaurant. Opened in the 1930s as the Club LaMaze, it has been Gazzari's Rock Club in recent years. 9039 Sunset.

5.   Marilyn Monroe and Joe DiMaggio Meet on Blind Date. It was here in 1953, at the former Villa Nova restaurant, that Marilyn and Joe first met on a blind date. In 1945, Vincente Minnelli proposed to Judy Garland while having dinner here. In past years it has been known as the Rainbow Bar & Grill. 9015 Sunset Blvd.

BEVERLY HILLS

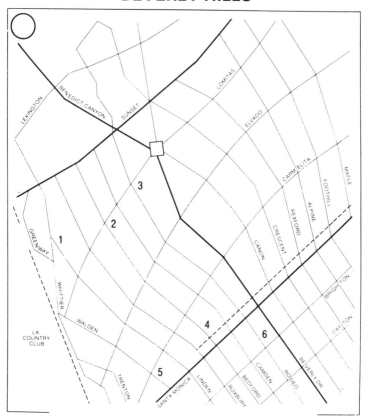

1. Gangster Bugsy Siegel Murdered. While sitting in the living room of this home in 1947, hoodlum Bugsy Siegel's head was almost blown off by the shotgun blasts that came through the windows. Siegel built the Flamingo Hotel in Las Vegas. 810 Linden Dr.

Home where gangster Bugsy Siegel was shot and killed.

BEVERLY HILLS

2. Lana Turner's Lover Stabbed to Death. In 1958, actress Lana Turner's teenage daughter, Cheryl Crane, stabbed to death gangster Johnny Stompanato here in the upstairs bedroom of Lana's Beverly Hills mansion. The killing of Stompanato, Lana's longtime boyfriend, was pronounced a justifiable homicide. Over thirty-five years later, it is still unknown whether Cheryl killed him in a jealous rage or in an attempt to save her mother's life. 730 N. Bedford.

3. Actress Kills Self After Marriage Rejection. Lupe Velez, whose star for many years blazed brilliantly in Hollywood, was found dead here in 1944 in a bedroom of her pink, Spanish-style home. Miss Velez, whose many romantic attachments during her lifetime included Gary Cooper, John Gilbert and Johnny Weissmuller, was a star who literally "burned up the road" in her overwhelming desire to "live" at any cost. Known as "Whoopee Lupe" and the "Mexican Spitfire," there have been few stars who, in real life, were so much like the roles they played as she. On the day that the pregnant Lupe was told by her lover, bit actor Harold Ramond, that he would not marry her, she went to her white-carpeted boudoir, wrote several suicide notes then swallowed a near full bottle of seconal tablets. She was found dead the next morning in her bed with its white silk sheets and pillow cases. Dressed in blue satin pajamas, she was lying as if asleep under an eiderdown quilt. She was 34. 732 N. Rodeo Dr.

4. Clara Bow/USC Football Team "Orgy." In her heyday, actress Clara Bow, known as the "It" girl, reportedly made love to John

Clara Bow

Gilbert, Gilbert Roland, Victor Fleming, Gary Cooper, Eddie Cantor, Bela "Dracula" Lugosi, and the entire University of Southern California football team. It was here in her home in 1927 that Clara entertained the "Thundering Herd"—USC's championship football squad. Neighbors and friends told tales of nude football game get-togethers on the front lawn, and drunken all-night orgies. Legend has it that the beautiful and tireless Clara introduced the team concept to lovemaking by taking on the entire team. Coach Howard Jones ended the spirited relationship with the popular actress by posting a sign in the USC locker room that read: "Clara Bow is off limits to all members of this football team." 512 N. Bedford.

5. "Witch's" House. Designed in 1921 by Harry Oliver, This "Hansel and Gretel" style house was originally built in Culver City as offices for the Irwin C. Willat movie studio. Moved here in the early 1930s, it is now a private residence. 516 Walden Dr.

6. Rodeo Drive. The "street-of-dreams" for the super-rich is two-and-one-half blocks long. 200-400 Rodeo Drive.

BEVERLY HILLS

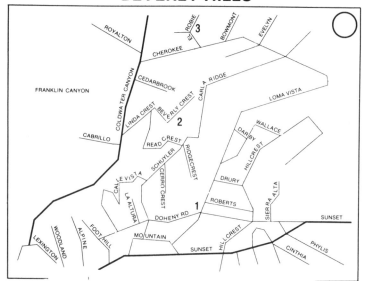

1. Greystone Mansion Scene of Doheny Murder/Suicide.
Millionaire oilman, E. L. Doheny built this 50-room mansion in 1928 at the cost of nine million dollars. Tragedy struck the home one year later in 1929, when Hugh Plunkett, private secretary to Doheny Jr., shot and killed the younger Doheny in one of its ornate rooms, then turned the gun on himself. Police reported Plunkett killed his employer after he was refused a raise. From 1969 to 1982, the mansion was the home of the American Film Institute. 501 N. Doheny.

2. Rock Hudson Dies of AIDS in "The Castle."
Hudson died here in a second floor bedroom of his home that he nicknamed "The Castle." After Hudson died of AIDS, at age 59, his body was cremated and his ashes scattered at sea. 9402 Beverly Crest Dr.

3. Mysterious Death of Actor Nick Adams.
When Adams died here in his home in 1968 from a drug overdose, Police found no syringes, medicine glasses, or pill bottles—nothing to indicate that his death was from anything but natural causes. Not known to have a drinking or drug problem, it was impossible to ascertain whether Adams' death was a suicide or accident. The coroner reported that the several sedatives and drugs that were found in his blood had probably killed him instantly. To this day, Police are still puzzled as to how the drugs had entered his system, as no means of ingestion were ever found near his body. He was 37 years old.

Nick Adams

Adams was best known for his starring roles in the television series *The Rebel,* and *Johnny Yuma.* 2126 El Roble Lane.

BEVERLY HILLS

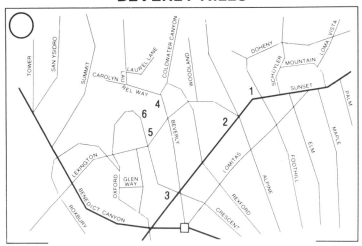

1. Mansion of Hollywood's "Boy Wonder." Built in 1918 by actress Pauline Fredericks, this mansion was the home of Irving Thalberg, Hollywood's top executive in the 1920s. Thalberg and actress Norma Shearer were married here in the backyard in 1927. Rudolph Valentino met his first wife here in 1919. 9419 Sunset.

2. Nude Statues of Sheik Al-Fassi. When Saudi Arabian Sheik Al-Fassi bought this 38-room mansion in 1978, he shocked Beverly Hills and created traffic jams when he painted the nude statues on the mansion's front veranda in natural skin tones, including both male and female private parts. Neighbors called the scene "a dirty Disneyland." Built in 1917, by M.H. Whittier, a co-founder of Beverly Hills, other former owners were S. Berch of Arden Farms and Leo Hartfield of the Hartfield-Zody chain. Gutted by fire in 1980, the sheik sold it in 1982. The mansion was razed in 1985. 9561 Sunset.

Nude statues of Sheik's former Sunset Blvd. mansion.

BEVERLY HILLS

The legendary Beverly Hills Hotel.

3.   The "Pink Palace." The Beverly Hills Hotel and bungalows, one of the world's havens for the rich and famous, was built in 1912 by oilman Burton Green. The hotel was constructed in a "T" shape and painted a shocking pink. In 1987, the Sultan of Brunei, one of the richest men in the world ($37 billion) bought the 260-room hotel for $185 million, $50 million more than oil baron Marvin Davis had paid for it a year earlier. The hotel was scheduled to close December 28, 1992 for a two-year $100 million-plus renovation. 9641 Sunset Blvd.

4.   Beverly Hills' Grandest Wedding Reception. When singer Johnny Ray was married in 1952, actress Marion Davies gave the wedding reception here in the backyard of her 27-room mansion. The affair was attended by over 1000, and was the grandest in Beverly Hills' history. Built in 1927 for over one million dollars, Miss Davies purchased the mansion in 1946 for a mere $125,000 and moved in with her boyfriend, William Randolph Hearst. In 1951, Hearst died here in his second floor bedroom. Miss Davies was living here when she died in 1961. 1011 N. Beverly Dr.

5.   Mansion of Studio Czar. Harry Cohn, probably the most feared and hated man in Hollywood, purchased this mansion in 1945. Built in the late 1920s, the home has nine bedrooms, seven baths, a theatre and three guest houses. After Cohn died in 1958, his widow married actor Laurence Harvey. In 1980 she sold the home to talk show host Mike Douglas. Douglas sold it in 1984. In 1988, the mansion was available as a rental for $35,000 per month. 1000 Crescent Dr.

6.   Carole Lombard Name Born. In 1924, when 16-year-old Jane Peters got her first movie role, she came here to tell a friend, Harry Lombard, about her good news and that the studio wanted to change her name. She asked Lombard's permission to use his last name. When she left that evening she left as Carole Lombard. The home was built in 1913 by Beverly Hills' first mayor, Silsby Spaulding. 1006 Crescent.

BEVERLY HILLS

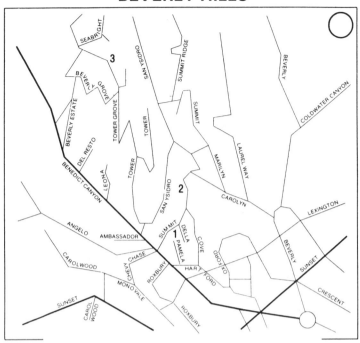

1.   Buster Keaton's X-Shaped Mansion. In the early 1920s, comedian Buster Keaton built this X-Shaped mansion—one of the showplaces of Beverly Hills. In 1927, when talkies came in, he lost the house, his fortune, and his career. When Fatty Arbuckle married in 1925, the wedding reception was held here. 1018 Pamela Dr.

2.   Pickfair Destroyed by Pia Zadora. When Douglas Fairbanks Sr. bought this site in 1918, it contained a small hunting lodge that was located way out in the wilderness. When Fairbanks and Mary Pickford moved into the lodge in 1920, a reporter named it "Pickfair." Their 100-foot swimming pool was the first in Beverly Hills. After her divorce from Fairbanks in 1936, Pickford married actor Buddy Rogers. The pair lived here until her death in 1979. Sports entrepreneur Jerry Buss purchased the 42-room mansion in 1980 for $5.4 million. In 1988, he sold it to singer Pia Zadora for $7 million, who, in 1990, leveled it to its foundations to build a larger home. 1143 Summit Drive.

3.   Love Nest of Greta Garbo and John Gilbert. Greta Garbo's love affair with John Gilbert in 1928 was compared to that of Romeo and Juliet, and Anthony and Cleopatra. It was here in Gilbert's hilltop mansion that the two lovers spent many hours together, and where Garbo took nude swims in the pool and long hikes in the hills. A silent screen idol, Gilbert's star faded when he could not adapt to sound. His career and romantic frustrations led him to heavy drinking. He died of a heart attack here in 1936, at age 41. Former tenants of the home were David O. Selznick/Jennifer Jones, and Elton John. The Spanish-style home was torn down in 1986. 1400 Tower Rd.

BEVERLY HILLS

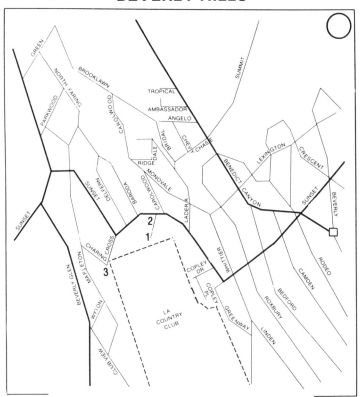

1.   Marilyn Monroe's 72-Year-Old Boyfriend. In 1950, at the beginning of her career, Marilyn Monroe lived in the guest house of this large estate. The occupant of the main house was Joseph M. Schenck, co-founder of 20th Century Fox Studios. During her stay here, Marilyn was at the "beck 'n call" of the 72-year-old Schenck and his desires. The mansion was built in the early 1920s by millionaire oilman, William M. Keck. In recent years, former owners have been Tony Curtis and Sonny & Cher. 141 S. Carolwood.

2.   Jayne Mansfield's Pink Mansion. After Jayne Mansfield bought this 18-room mansion in the early 1960s, she had it painted pink, then built a heart-shaped pool with an inscription on the bottom that read, "I love you Jaynie." In 1932. singer Rudy Vallee purchased the spanish-style home for $100.000 cash and named it "Three Palms." Singer Englebert Humperdinck bought the home in 1978 for $2 million. In 1990, he offered it for sale for $8 million. 10100 Sunset.

3.   Playboy Mansion. In 1927, Arthur Letts Jr., whose father founded both the Broadway and Bullock's stores, built this 23-room English stone manor. The mansion has 18-inch walls, a Botticini marble entryway floor, and an Aeolian pipe organ built into a wall. In 1971, Hugh Hefner purchased the six-acre estate and converted it into Playboy Mansion West. 10236 Charing Cross Rd.

BEVERLY HILLS

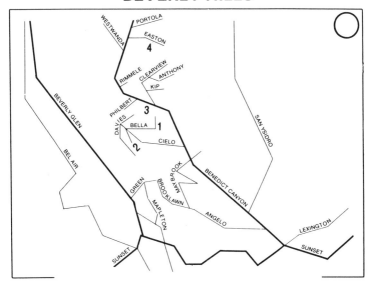

1.   Rudolph Valentino's Falcon Lair. When Valentino purchased this 16-room mansion in 1925 for $175,000, he promptly named it "Falcon Lair" after a movie he was planning, but never made, "The Hooded Falcon" When his actress/wife, Natacha Rambova left him at this time, he moved into the house by himself. In 1926, after living in the mansion for less than a year—Valentino died. To pay off his many debts, Falcon Lair was auctioned off for $145,000—but its new owner never moved into it. The home, built in 1923, stood empty for eight years until it was sold again in 1934 for $18,000! Former owners were conductor Werner Janssen and his actress/wife, Ann Harding. In 1953, actress Gloria Swanson rented it just before it was purchased by its recent owner, tobacco heiress, Doris Duke. 1436 Bella Dr.

"Falcon Lair," Valentino's fabled Beverly Hills mansion.

BEVERLY HILLS

2.   Sharon Tate Murdered by Manson Gang. On August 9th, 1969, actress Sharon Tate, Abigal Folger, Jay Sebring, and two others were butchered here by the Charles Manson gang. 10050 Cielo Dr.

3.   Murder or Suicide? of George "Superman" Reeves. In 1951, George Reeves was world famous for his portrayal of television's "Superman." Eight years later, in 1959, Reeves, 45, was found dead on the floor of his bedroom here—he had been shot in the head. A gun lay on the floor between his legs. The coroner ruled his death a suicide, the result of despondency over the slump in his career. Claiming that he was murdered, Reeves' mother shipped his body back east. Rumors circulated that she put his body on "ice" until she could prove he did not kill himself. Many persons in Hollywood believe today, that his body is still on "ice." Reeves lay unburied in the east for eight months until he was cremated and his ashes returned to Los Angeles and placed secretly in an unmarked urn in a local cemetery. His mother died in 1964, still trying to prove he was murdered. Former occupants report they moved because of the ghostly incidents inside the house. 1579 Benedict Canyon.

4.   Jean Harlow's Husband a Suicide or Murder? Jean Harlow was America's sex symbol when she wed director Paul Bern in 1932. Two months after the marriage, Bern committed suicide here in his Bavarian-style home by shooting himself while in Harlow's bedroom. Harlow, and Bern's former lover were at one time suspect's in his death. In 1968, the "jinxed" home was purchased by hair stylist, Jay Sebring because of its "far-out" reputation. In 1969, just down the canyon, Sebring was murdered along with Sharon Tate. The home has unusual rain gutters. At the end of each gutter is a hand-carved, head-sized, wooden likeness of silent screen stars Rudolph Valentino, Douglas Fairbanks Sr., and Mary Pickford. 9820 Easton Dr.

Jean Harlow-Paul Bern "jinxed" Benedict Canyon home.

BEVERLY HILLS - WESTWOOD

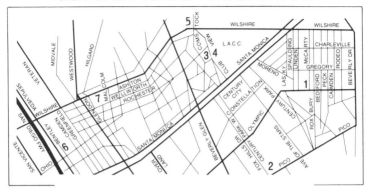

1.   Actress Pier Angeli Dies of Drug Overdose. When actor James Dean asked Angeli to marry him in 1954, she declined, then broke Dean's heart when she married singer Vic Damone. In 1971, at age 39, she died here of a drug overdose. 355 S. McCarty Dr.

2.   20th Century Fox Studios. This studio was formed in 1935 when Twentieth Century and Fox Films merged. 10201 W. Pico.

3.   Jean Harlow Haunts Her Former Home. The day after Jean Harlow's husband Paul Bern committed suicide in 1932, Harlow tried to kill herself here. The pair were married here in the living room. Former owners of the home report that Harlow haunted the house while they lived there. 1353 Clubview Dr.

4.   Rin-Tin-Tin Dies in Arms of Jean Harlow. The dog star died here in 1932 while Harlow cradled his head in her arms. Celebrities attended the services and burial in the backyard. 1352 Clubview Dr.

5.   Comedian Freddie Prinze Kills Self. Reportedly obsessed with comedian Lenny Bruce who died in 1966 of a drug overdose, Prinze, former star of the TV series *Chico and the Man,* would tell his friends "What a terrific life to die young and be a legend." His idol was comedian Lenny Bruce, and he believed was Bruce reincarnated. In 1977, despondent over a separation from his wife, Prinze put a gun to his head here in his apartment—then pulled the trigger. He was 22. In 1983, his death was ruled an accident. 865-75 Comstock.

6.   Actress Gail Russell Dies Surrounded by Liquor Bottles. Russell was a movie star at 18 and a has-been at 30. Once voted the "star of tomorrow," she was an insecure introvert who suffered from stage fright. Her inability to cope with the pressures of Hollywood drove her to alcoholism. In the early 1950s, she was involved in a romantic scandal with John Wayne, and after her divorce from actor Guy Madison in 1954, her drinking got worse and film work became scarce. In 1961, she was found dead of "natural causes" here in her home. An empty vodka bottle was by her side on the floor where she had fallen from a couch. She was 36. 1436 Bentley.

7.   Westwood Memorial Cemetery. The final resting place of Marilyn Monroe and Natalie Wood. 1218 Glendon Ave.

WESTWOOD

WESTWOOD MEMORIAL CEMETERY

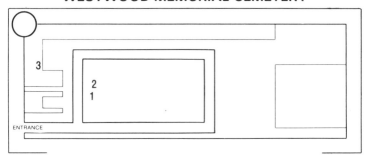

1.   Natalie Wood. When actress Natalie Wood was buried here beneath a shady camphor tree, just across the road from the crypt of Marilyn Monroe, a balalaika player strummed Russian melodies beside her biege-colored coffin that was covered with 450 white gardenias worked into a candlelight lace. The out-of-season gardenias had to be obtained from eight states. Wood, who was married to actor Robert Wagner, was found floating in the ocean at Santa Catalina Island's Isthmus Cove in 1981. She apparently slipped and drowned accendentally while trying to enter a small boat while leaving her yacht. Her cries for help went unheard. She was 43.

2.   Richard Conte Coming Back in Another Life? Conte's gravestone here is the most unusual in Hollywood. His plaque, near Natalie Wood, contains several references of a world far beyond the grave. There are small pyramids in each corner of the marker—but the most unusual feature is the question mark that follows the date of his death. Did Conte expect to come back in another life? A leading man in the 1940s and 50s, Conte, 65, was often seen in the role of an Italian- American cop or gangster. He died of a heart attack in 1975.

Unusual grave marker of multi-talented Richard Conte.

WESTWOOD

WESTWOOD MEMORIAL CEMETERY

3.   Marilyn Monroe. Marilyn Monroe's simple wall crypt here in the Corridor of Memories is visited by more people than any other Hollywood star grave. When Marilyn died in 1962, her body lay unclaimed in the county morgue until her former husband, baseball star, Joe DiMaggio arranged to have it moved here for burial. He chose this tiny, secluded cemetery for her final resting place because several of her relatives are also buried here. On the night before the funeral, the grief-stricken DiMaggio sat up all night next to Marilyn's

Marilyn Monroe

open coffin. The next day, fewer than twenty people were invited to attend the services in the cemetery's small chapel—DiMaggio had barred all Marilyn's Hollywood friends. He also declared that her casket would be kept closed—no one would be able to view her remains. The casket was then placed in an outdoor wall storage vault where the former film queen was laid to rest. Years later, an unsuccessful attempt was made to break into her sealed crypt. It was rumored that the

robbers were after a necklace that Marilyn was wearing when she was entombed. Cemetery officials confirmed the break-in attempt, but added that she lies behind almost two feet of concrete. When the crypt next to Marilyn was sold several years ago, there was speculation that the purchaser was Joe DiMaggio. DiMaggio's 20-year-ritual of having six red roses placed on her crypt three times a week was ended in 1982. Monroe, 36, died of a drug overdose on August 5, 1962.

Simple outdoor wall crypt of Marilyn Monroe.

BEL AIR

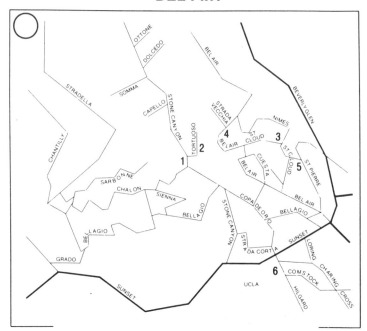

1.   Bel Air Hotel. Built in the 1920s by Alphonzo Bell, the 66-room hotel is the country club of deluxe hotels in the Los Angeles area. The Bel Air was the home of actress Grace Kelly during her Hollywood movie career. 701 Stone Canyon Rd.

2.   Kim Novak/Sammy Davis Jr. Love Nest. Actress Kim Novak paid $95,000 for this home in the 1950s. She had a fall-out shelter built in the backyard during the atomic war scare. Sammy Davis Jr. came here often during their love affair. 780 Tortuoso Way.

3.   President Reagan's Retirement Home. Before the Reagan's moved into this $2.5 million "fixer-upper" in 1989, it was known as the "Demon house" because its address was 666. Nancy had the address changed to 668 before moving in. 668 St. Cloud.

4.   Beverly Hillbillies Mansion. Built in 1935 at a cost of $2 million by Hoover Dam engineer, Lyn Atkinson whose wife refused to move in because she thought the 40-room mansion was too pretentious, so he sold it to hotel magnate Arnold Kirkeby for $200,000. Used as the Clampett home in the TV show "The Beverly Hillbillies," it sold in 1986 for $13.6 million. 750 Bel Air.

5.   Errol Flynn Accused of Rape. It was here in a second floor bedroom of this home in 1942, that actor Errol Flynn was accused of raping seventeen-year-old, would-be-actress, Betty Hansen. Flynn was acquitted of the charge. Silent screen actress Colleen Moore built the 16-room mansion in 1927. 345 St. Pierre Rd.

6.   UCLA. Built on the site of the historic Wolfskill Rancho, UCLA has been located here since 1929. 405 Hilgard.

BRENTWOOD

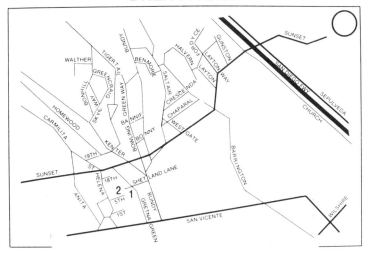

1. Former Home of Raymond Chandler. Creator of the fictional private eye Philip Marlow, Chandler wrote "High Window" and "Lady in the Lake" while here in the 1940s. 12216 Shetland Lane.

2. Marilyn Monroe Found Dead—Murder or Suicide? On the morning of August 5, 1962, actress Marilyn Monroe, 36, was found dead here in the bedroom of her home. Her nude body was lying face down on the bed, her hand was on the telephone—her finger still on the dial. The coroner ruled her death a probable suicide—she had swallowed 47 tablets of Nembutal, a sleeping sedative. The first police officer on the scene charges that Marilyn was murdered. In late 1982, the L.A. District Attorney, after a three-month investigation concluded that Marilyn died of a drug overdose that could have been either a suicide or accidental—not murder, adding, "I hope that Marilyn Monroe will now be permitted to rest in peace." 12305 Fifth Helena.

The window on the right is the bedroom where Marilyn Monroe died.

BRENTWOOD - PACIFIC PALISADES

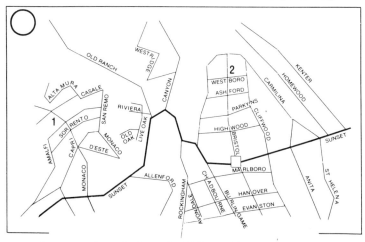

1.   Actress Carole Landis Kills Self Over Rex Harrison.
Landis rose to fame in the 1940 film *One Million B.C.* She was the
screens' original "Sweater Girl." In 1948, her love affair with Rex
Harrison ended when he would not marry her. With her career on the
skids and her big romance burned out, she swallowed a bottleful of
seconal tablet here in her home. Harrison discovered her body on the
floor of the bathroom. She was 29. 1465 Capri Dr.

2.   Joan Crawford's "Mommie Dearest" House. Crawford
bought this home shortly before she married actor Douglas Fairbanks
Jr. in 1929. They named it "El Jodo." At one time in the 1940s,
Crawford removed all the bathtubs from the home, saying that "it was
unsanitary to sit in one's bathwater" In 1978, her daughter Christina,
in her book *Mommie Dearest,* told of growing up here in a nightmare
of alcohoism, abuse and terror. Former owners have been actor Donald
O'Conner and entrepreneur Gary Berwin. 426 N. Bristol.

Brentwood home where Joan Crawford removed all bathtubs.

PACIFIC PALISADES - SANTA MONICA

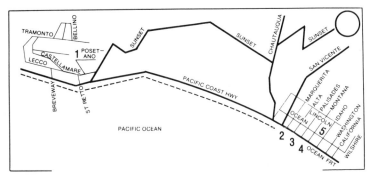

1.   Mysterious Murder-Suicide? of Actress Thelma Todd.
Did Thelma Todd kill herself? Was she murdered? Or was her death an accident? A vivacious blonde comedienne, Miss Todd, who appeared in many film comedies in the 1920s and 30s, was found dead under mysterious circumstances here in this small garage in December of 1935. She was slumped over the steering wheel of her new Packard convertible, her face covered with blood. There was blood splattered all around Thelma on the seat, and the running board. Police called her death a suicide. Thelma's lawyer claimed she was murdered. An autopsy showed she died of carbon monoxide poisoning, and a coroner's jury ruled her death an accident. Miss Todd, 30, lived in an apartment above the restaurant she owned at 17575 Pacific Coast Highway, just down the hill from where she was found. Her strange death is still one of Hollywood's most baffling. 17531 Posetano Rd.

2.   Site of Marion Davies' 118-Room Mansion. In 1928, William Randolph Hearst built a mansion on this site for his girlfriend, actress Marion Davies. "Ocean House" contained 118 rooms, 55 baths, and 37 fireplaces. Many rooms, some dating back to the 10th century, were imported from Europe for reassembly here on the beach. The mansion was destroyed in the late 50s. The servants quarters, and a guest house are all that remain. The property has been used as a private club in recent years. 415 Palisades Beach Rd.

3.   Secret Rendezvous of Marilyn Monroe and JFK. It was here in this beach home during 1960-61 that Marilyn Monroe and President John F. Kennedy met secretly during their love affair. The home was owned at the time by Kennedy's brother-in-law, actor Peter Lawford. Former MGM Studio vice-president, Louis B. Mayer, owned the mansion from 1925 to 1957. 625 Palisades Beach Rd.

4.   Douglas Fairbanks' Ocean-Front Mansion. Fairbanks, a silent screen star, and once married to actress Mary Pickford, died here in his beach home in 1939 of a heart attack. Before burial, his body lay in state here in an ornately-carved bed in front of a window that overlooked the ocean. Fairbanks' 150-pound mastiff whined beside the death bed for hours—refusing to move. 705 Palisades Beach.

5.   Last Home of Comedian Stan Laurel. Laurel died here in his small apartment in 1965 at age 75. 849 Ocean Ave.

CULVER CITY - BALDWIN HILLS

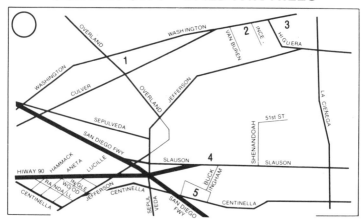

1. Studio of the Stars. Built in 1915 as the Triangle Studios by D.W. Griffith, Mack Sennett and Tom Ince. Owned by Sam Goldwyn in 1918, it became Metro Goldwyn Mayer in 1924. Columbia bought it from Lorimar in 1989. 10202 Washington Blvd.

2. Gone With the Wind Studio. Built in 1918 by Tom Ince, this studio has had many name changes: Pathe (1924), DeMille (1925), RKO-Pathe (1931), Selznick (1935), Desilu-Culver (1957), and in recent years, Culver Studios. The films, *King of Kings, King Kong, Gone With the Wind,* and the first "Our Gang" comedies were made here. The administrative building is an exact replica of George Washington's home, Mount Vernon. Columbia Studios paid $80 million for the 17-acre, 14-sound stage studio in 1991. 9336 Washington.

Studio office building a replica of George Washington's home.

3. Our Gang Studios. The former Hal Roach Studios where the "Our Gang" comedies were filmed in the 1930s and 40s, was located here until it was razed in the 1950s. 8822 Washington.

4. Holy Cross Cemetery. 5835 Slauson Ave.

5. Hillside Memorial Park Cemetery. 6001 Centinela Ave.

BALDWIN HILLS

HOLY CROSS CEMETERY

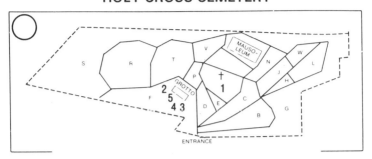

1. **Rosalind Russell.** Russell was nominated for four Academy Awards including *Auntie Mame* in 1958. She died of cancer in 1976 at 63. Her monument is in section M in front of the large cross.

2. **Charles Boyer.** One of the screen's greatest lovers, Boyer committed suicide two days after his wife of 44 years died in 1978. Boyer was 78 when he took his own life with an overdose of seconal tablets. In the grave next to Boyer and his wife is their son Michael, who killed himself in 1965. He was 21.

3. **Bela "Dracula" Lugosi.** Actor Bela Lugosi starred in many horror films during the 1930s and 40s. His most famous role was that of Count Dracula in the 1930 film *Dracula*. He was 71 when he died of a heart attack in 1956. His grave is just to the right of Bing Crosby. As he requested, he was buried in his Dracula cape.

4. **Bing Crosby.** Crosby is buried next to his first wife Dixie and his parents. He died of a heart attack in 1977 in Spain. He was 73.

The plain and simple grave of crooner Bing Crosby.

BALDWIN HILLS

HOLY CROSS CEMETERY

Grave of actress Sharon Tate and her unborn son Paul.

5. Sharon Tate. In 1967, actress Sharon Tate's film career was on the rise. Married to actor-director Ramon Polanski, she had starred in the film *The Valley of the Dolls.* In 1968, Miss Tate and her unborn baby were murdered by the Manson gang (see page 54). She was 26.

MAIN MAUSOLEUM

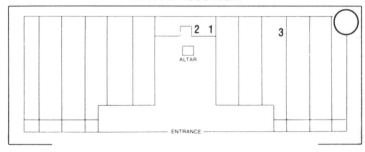

1. Mario Lanza the American Caruso. Lanza was called the next "Caruso" during the 1950s. But an arrogant personality, an alcohol problem, and a fight against obesity helped ruin his career. He died of a "heart attack" at age 38 in 1959. Friends believe that he was killed by the Mafia. His wife died of a drug overdose five months after his death. His crypt is just to the right of the altar.

2. Joan Davis. A movie and TV comedienne in the 1940s and 50s, Davis died of a heart attack in 1961. She was 53. Her crypt is to the left of Mario Lanza.

3. Spike Jones. Leader of the 1940s band "The City Slickers," Jones, died of emphysema in 1965, at 54. Row 70 near the top.

BALDWIN HILLS

HILLSIDE CEMETERY

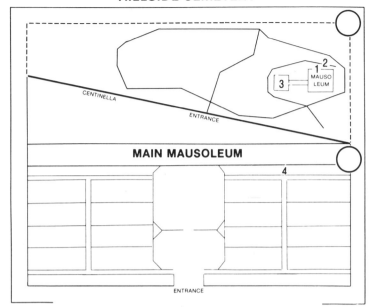

1. **Michael Landon.** "Little Joe" of the TV series *Bonanza.* Landon died in 1991 of cancer. Enter main entrance and go straight ahead through lobby and court to the family rooms on the left. His family room is opposite the first side entrance of the mausoleum.

2. **Lorne Greene.** Star of *Bonanza,* Greene died of pneumonia in 1987. Follow walkway to right of Landon to the outside. His flat marker is on the left lawn and to the right of a bench and a headstone with the name Marx, opposite a doorway behind the mausoleum.

3. **Al Jolson.** Jolson died in 1950 of a heart attack. He was 64. His monument is on the hill just to the right of the cemetery entrance,

4. **Jack Benny.** Benny, 80, died of cancer in 1974. His crypt is at the end the Hall of Graciousness in the main mausoleum.

Statue of Al Jolson kneels to the right of his self-designed monument.

LOS ANGELES

1. **Los Angeles Memorial Coliseum.** The 105,000 seat stadium was built for the 1932 world Olympics. Exposition Park.

2. **University of Southern California.** Hoover & Exposition.

3. **Home of Comedian "Fatty" Arbuckle.** Built in 1907, by Captain Randolph F. Miner, this was the home of comedian "Fatty" Arbuckle when he was arrested for the rape-murder of actress Virginia Rappe in 1921. Arbuckle lived here during the entire trial. Other famous owners of the home were actresses Theda Bara, 1918; Miriam Cooper, 1923; and Norma Talmadge and her director husband, Joseph Schenck in 1924. The mansion has been the home for Catholic priests in recent years. 649 W. Adams Blvd.

4. **Birthplace of Adlai E. Stevenson.** Ex-Presidential candidate, Stevenson was born in this home in 1900. 2639 Monmouth.

5. **Judy Garland Home in 1929.** Judy Garland (then 7-year-old Francis Gumm) her mother and sisters were living here in an upstairs back apartment in 1929. 1814½ S. Orchard.

Wall marker of Michael Landon.

Elizabeth Short, the "Black Dahlia"

6.   Murder of the Black Dahlia. The butchered nude body of a young woman, neatly cut in half at the waist, was found lying in the weeds here on January 15, 1947. Her slashed breasts were covered with cigarette burns, her mouth had been slit with a knife three inches on each side while she was still alive, and there was a deep triangle gouge in her left thigh where there was once a rose tattoo. The hunk of flesh with the tattoo was discovered during the autopsy, inserted inside her body. Rope burns on her wrists, ankles and neck indicated that she had been tortured for several days. After he killed her, the killer dissected the body, drained it of all blood, washed the pieces, shampooed and carefully set the hair, then laid out the pieces here (just west of the sidewalk) in what was then empty lots used as a "lovers' lane." The victim was identified as Elizabeth "Betty" Short, 22, a waitress, and would-be-actress who loved to prowl Hollywood Boulevard. Friends nick-named her the "Black Dahlia" because of the flower-like arrangement of her dyed jet black hair and her liking for black clothing. More than 40 persons have confessed to the unsolved murder. The spot where her severed body was found is a few feet west of the sidewalk into the driveway in front of 3925 S. Norton.

LOS ANGELES

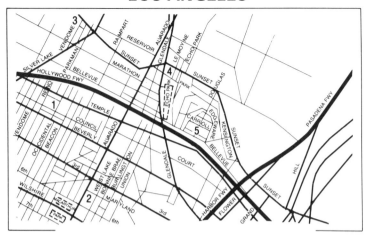

1. Oldest Movie Studio in Hollywood. The Bosworth-Morosco Studios, built in 1913 by actor Hobart Bosworth is the oldest studio in L.A. It was once owned by the Famous Players-Lasky Studios. The small studio was still active in 1992. 201 N. Occidental.

2. Hollywood's First Murder Scandal. Director William Desmond Taylor was one of Hollywood's most colorful personalities. The 45-year old, handsome man-about-town was known for his associations with young, pretty actresses. In 1922, the career of the adventurous Taylor came to an end when he was found dead here in his bungalow. He was discovered lying on his back on the living room floor—his open eyes staring at the ceiling. He was laid out like a department store wax dummy—too perfect, too immaculate. The first doctor on the scene declared that he had died of a gastric hemorrhage. But when the police rolled his body over, they found a bullet hole in his back—Taylor had become the victim of Hollywood's first murder scandal. Among the many suspects were two of his young girlfriends, actresses Mabel Normand and Mary Miles Minter, and Miss Minter's mother, Mrs. Charlotte Shelby. No arrests were ever made and the murder is still unsolved. The court was torn down in the 1950s, and the site is now a parking lot. 404 S. Alvarado.

3. Laurel & Hardy Piano Stairway. In 1932, Laurel & Hardy made a comedy film called *The Music Box* in which the pair attempted to deliver a piano to a home located at the top of a very long flight of stairs. The stairway used in the film remains unchanged just south of Sunset Blvd. 923-27 Vendome St.

4.   Sister Aimee's Temple. Angelus Four Square Temple was built in 1923 by evangelist, Aimee Semple McPherson. 1100 Glendale.

5.   Street of Vintage Victorian Homes. Carroll Avenue, on top of once fashionable Angelino Heights, is one of the last remnants of Los Angeles of the 1800s. This one block of beautiful victorian homes is a must for vintage house buffs. 1300 Carroll Ave.

LOS ANGELES - DOWNTOWN

1.   Los Angeles Convention Center. 1201 S. Figueroa.

2.   United Artists Theatre. Designed in the French-New Orleans style, this beautiful movie house still has the murals of Mary Pickford and Douglas Fairbanks Sr. on its walls. 933 S. Broadway.

3.   Produce Market. Wholesale supplier of fresh fruits and vegetables to Los Angeles food markets. 9th & San Pedro.

4.   Flower Market. One of the largest fresh flower markets in the country with over 400 growers. 766 Wall.

5.   Garment Center. Manufacturer's outlets of famous brand clothing at wholesale prices to the public. 700-800 Los Angeles St.

6.   First Movie Studio in Los Angeles. Early in 1909, film producer William N. Selig arrived from New York and opened the first "movie-studio" in Los Angeles when he rented an old mansion that was located here. Selig immediately put into production the first movie ever to be filmed in its entirety in California. He also built the first motion-picture set when he set up interior sets in the backyard. Selig's first film was In the *Sultan's Power* starring Hobart Bosworth and directed by Francis Boggs. A few months after completion of the film, Boggs was shot and killed here in front of the studio. In 1923, while recalling the historic event, Bosworth lamented, "the house is gone, it is a parking station now, but someday, I imagine, the site will be marked by a brass plate." Over seventy years later, the site is still a parking lot, and the "brass plate" has never been put up. 751 S. Olive.

LOS ANGELES - DOWNTOWN

7.   Best Preserved Movie Theatre in Los Angeles. Opened in 1926, the Orpheum Theatre is the best preserved of the downtown theatres. Its gold-leaf ceiling, oak paneling, gothic arches and art-deco furniture are worth seeing. 842 S. Broadway.

8.   Los Angeles Hilton Hotel. 930 Wilshire Blvd.

9.   Murder-Suicide of Star Vaudeville Act. The former Pantages Theatre here was the scene of tragedy in 1923 when two members of a star act were killed just before show time. The headlining act was an Oriental group of five mystic Chinamen who called themselves the "Choy Ling Foo Troupe." The group, who had entertained millions all over the world, were in their dressing room preparing to go on stage, when they became involved in a heated argument. As the audience squirmed restlessly in their seats, awaiting the group's appearance in the theatre above, Choy Den, the fire-eater, shot and killed his cousin, Choy You Chung, the contortionist. Then true to the tradition of his ancestors, he placed the gun to his head and fired. In 1929, Alexander Pantages, head of the Pantages Theatres, became involved in one of L.A:s most sensational trials when he was accused of raping a 17-year-old schoolgirl here in his second-floor office. Built in 1920, the theatre was known as the Warner's in the 1940s. The converted theatre is now the Jewelry Mart. 607 S. Hill.

10.   Most Beautiful Theatre in Los Angeles. Built in the French Renaissance style of Louis XIV, the Los Angeles Theatre opened in 1931 with such luxury items as electric cigarette lighters, an art gallery, a threetiered crystal fountain at the head of the grand staircase, and a mahogany paneled ballroom. It was once described as the most beautiful theatre in the world. 615 So. Broadway.

11.   Alexandria Hotel. When opened in 1906, the 500-room Alexandria Hotel was considered the most elegant in L.A. The hotel's restaurant still has its Tiffany glass skylights. 501 So. Spring.

12.   Ghost Hotel. When the Alexandria Hotel was built in 1906, an adjacent eight-story building was built as a 55-room annex. Designed as a part of the Alexandria, it had no stairs or elevators to take its guests to their rooms, so its patrons used the Alexandria's elevators. In 1934, the annex was closed. In 1937, after a disagreement between the two owners, the hallways between the two buildings were bricked up—thus sealing off access to the 55 rooms. After almost 60 years without a paying guest, the hallways remain bricked up, ceilings are sagging, windows are boarded up, and rooms are littered with trash. The only guests of the once elegant, but now "ghostly" hotel, are the rats that scurry from room to room. 218 W. 5th.

13.   Biltmore Hotel. Called the finest hotel in the country when it was opened in 1923. 530 W. 5th St.

14.   Los Angeles Public Library. 630 W. 5th.

15.   Arco-Plaza. L.A's first underground mall. 505 S. Flower.

LOS ANGELES - DOWNTOWN

16.   Bonaventure Hotel, Built in 1976. 5th and Figueroa.

17.   World Trade Center. Items from nearly every country in the world are featured here. 333 S. Flower.

18.   Angel's Flight. The former site of the world's shortest railroad. The unique little two-car railway that once carried residents to their homes that were located at the top of Bunker Hill was destroyed in 1969. Today, a huge apartment complex sits on the site—no trace of railroad exists. NW corner of Third & Hill.

19.   Grand Central Market. Founded in 1917, this busy market of over 50 stalls features various ethnic foods. 317 So. Broadway.

20.   Million Dollar Theatre. Built in 1918 by Sid Grauman, the theatre is one of the most impressive movie palaces in the country. Has sculptured gargoyles and moorish carvings. 307 S. Broadway.

21.   Broadway's Architectural Surprise. The inside of this 1893 building is famous for its central court with elegant wrought-iron stairwells, ornamental balconies with railings imported from France, two open-cage elevators, and its light which is diffused by its overhead skylight. Sometimes called L. A.'s "most pleasant surprise," it is one the area's remarkable architectural achievements. 304 S. Broadway.

22.   Music Center. The Dorothy Chandler Pavilion, Mark Taper Forum, and Ahmanson Theatre are located here. 135 N. Grand.

23.   New Otani Hotel. 120 Los Angeles St.

24.   Little Tokyo. First & San Pedro Streets.

25.   Los Angeles City Hall. 200 N. Spring St.

26.   Forgotten Birthplace of Los Angeles. It was on this site that Los Angeles was founded in 1781 when a small group of 44 settlers entered the new Plaza, marched slowly around the square, then stood in a circle while the Spanish Governor gave it the name "Pueblo of the Queen of the Angels," and asked for a blessing for the new town. As the town grew, this original site was neglected, and eventually the entire square and its old adobes were obliterated. When the Plaza was re-located across the street on the east side of Main St, the original site was forgotten and became part of a lowly section of the city called Sonoratown. Today, there is no trace of the original Plaza, nor is there a plaque to mark the historical site which is now buried under a large parking lot. 600 block of North Main St.

27.   Olvera Street. Located next to the new Plaza, Olvera Street is said to be the oldest street in Los Angeles. One of Southern California' biggest tourist attractions, it is now a Mexican marketplace of colorful shops and cafes. 400-500 N. Main.

28.   Union Station. Built in 1939 on part of the original Chinatown site, it still has beautiful ceilings and ornate paneling. 800 N. Alameda.

29.   Chinatown. Has been located here since 1930. 900 Broadway.

SILVER LAKE - GLENDALE

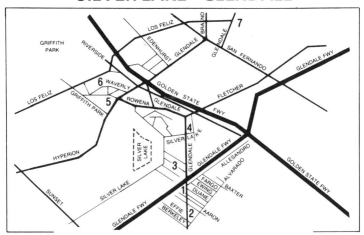

1. Selig Studio. In 1909, William N. Selig built his movie studio here in an area then known as Edendale. In 1916, Selig sold the little studio to Fox Studios. In later years the lot was known as the Garson Studios, Hollywood Studios, and Snub Pollard Studios. The studio was razed in the 1940s. 1845 Glendale.

2. Mack Sennett's Keystone Kops. When Charles Bauman and Adam Kessel arrived in Hollywood in 1909, they built the Bison Studios here where western films were made. Mack Sennett bought the lot in 1912 and named it Keystone, where he filmed the "Keystone Kops" comedies. In 1913, the first custard pie ever thrown in a movie, was tossed here by Mabel Normand into Ben Turpin's face. Charlie Chaplin, "Fatty" Arbuckle, and Gloria Swanson began their film careers here. Sennett abandoned the studio in 1928. Only one sound stage remains and it is now a self-storage facility. 1712 Glendale.

3. Steepest Street in Los Angeles. In 1932, lofty Fargo Street was used by Olympic runners to train on. 2000 Fargo St.

4. Tom Mix Horse Buried Under Bank Parking Lot? In 1914, William Selig built a western town here complete with saloon, western store and jail, and named it "Mixville" after his cowboy star, Tom Mix, who made his films here. Selig sold the town-ranch to Fox Studios in 1916. No trace of the ranch remains today. It is rumored that Mix's first horse, "Old Blue" is buried beneath the parking lot of a bank on the old Mixville site. 2450 Glendale.

5. First Mickey Mouse Cartoon Made. Walt Disney built his first studio here in 1926. It was here that the first Mickey Mouse cartoon *Plane Crazy* was made. *Snow White and the Seven Dwarfs* was made here in 1937. Disney left here for Burbank in 1940 and the site is now a market and parking lot. 2719 Hyperion.

6. Manson Murder Victims. Leno and Rosemary LaBianca were murdered here in 1969 by the Manson Gang. 3301 Waverly.

7. Forest Lawn Cemetery. 1712 S. Glendale.

GLENDALE
FOREST LAWN CEMETERY

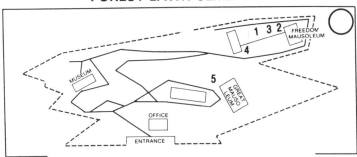

1.   Sammy Davis Jr. After Davis died of cancer at age 64 in 1990, he was reportedly buried wearing his Bojangles cuff links and a watch given to him on his death bed by Frank Sinatra. His grave is behind the walls of section just to the right of entrance of Garden of Honor.

2.   Walt Disney. Disney, 65, died of cancer in 1966. His ashes are in a corner garden to the left of the Freedom Mausoleum entrance.

3.   Errol Flynn. Although Flynn died in 1959, his grave was unmarked until 1979. It is rumored that he was buried with six bottles of whiskey placed there by drinking cronies. He died of a heart attack at age 50. His flat marker is in front of a small bronze statue.

4.   Casey Stengel. The former baseball manager died in 1975. He was 85. His marker is to the left of the Court of Freedom statues.

5. Aimee Semple McPherson. The world famous evangelist who founded the Foursquare Foursquare Church died in 1944 of an overdose of sleeping pills. She was 53. It is rumored that Sister Aimee was interred with a live telephone beside her. Her large monument is to the left of and down the hill from Great Mausoleum entrance.

Kneeling angels guard tomb of Aimee Semple McPherson.

GLENDALE

FOREST LAWN CEMETERY

FREEDOM HALL MAUSOLEUM (1st floor)

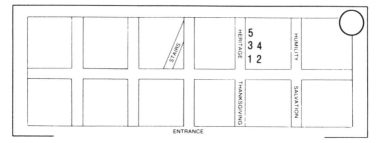

1. Alan Ladd. Pint-sized tough-guy, Ladd, 50, died in 1964 under mysterious circumstances. His death was ruled the result of an overdose of sedatives mixed with alcohol. Fourteen months earlier, he was nearly killed by an "accidental" self-inflicted gun-shot wound. A bust of Ladd sets in front of his crypt in the Sanctuary of Heritage.

2. Nat "King" Cole. Singer-pianist, Cole, 45, died in l965 of lung cancer. His crypt is in the Sanctuary of Heritage.

3. Jeanette MacDonald. A concert singer and actress in the 1930s and 40s, Miss MacDonald and Nelson Eddy were a popular musical film team. She died of a heart attack at age 59 in 1965.

4. "It" Girl Clara Bow. Clara Bow became famous as the girl with "It" after she starred in the 1927 movie "It." In the crypt next to her is her former husband, actor and ex-Lieutenant Governor of Nevada, Rex Bell. Plagued with a nerve condition in her later years, Miss Bow died of a heart attack in 1965. She was 60.

5. Gracie Allen. The wife of comedian George Burns, Gracie died of a heart attack in 1964. She was 58,

Bust of Alan Ladd sits to the left of his autographed wall crypt.

GLENDALE

FOREST LAWN CEMETERY
FREEDOM HALL MAUSOLEUM (1st floor)

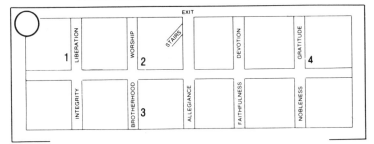

1.   Larry Fine of the Three Stooges. A member of the original Three Stooges, Fine died of a stroke in 1975 at age 64. His crypt is in the Sanctuary of Liberation near the bottom.

2.   Chico Marx. The piano playing member of the Marx comedy team who always spoke with an Italian accent, died of a heart attack at 71 in 1961. His crypt is in the Sanctuary of Worship.

3.   Gummo Marx. An early member of the Marx Brothers, Gummo never appeared before the cameras. He quit the act in the early 1920s to become the team's agent and business manager. He died in 1977 at age 85. Sanctuary of Brotherhood near the bottom.

4.   King of the Movies. A star in the silent era, Francis X. Bushman was known as the "handsomest man in the movies." His epithet reads: "The king of the movies." He died in 1966 of a heart attack at 83. He is in the Sanctuary of Gratitude near the top.

THE GREAT MAUSOLEUM

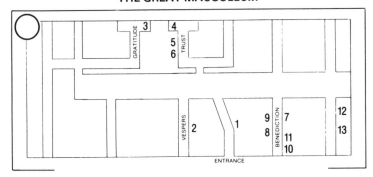

1.   The Dolly Sisters. Identical twins, Jenny and Rosie Dolly were a world famous dancing act from 1909 to 1924. In 1941, Jenny hanged herself at age 48 (see page 9). Rosie, 78, died of heart failure in 1970. Their crypts are on the right after entering the the mausoleum.

2.   Crooner Russ Columbo. In the early 1930s, Columbo and Bing Crosby were the top "crooners" in the country. He was accidentally shot and killed in 1934. Sanctuary of Vespers.

GLENDALE

FOREST LAWN CEMETERY

THE GREAT MAUSOLEUM

3.   Phillip K. Wrigley. The founder of Wrigley's chewing gum. The Wrigley niche is at the end of the Sanctuary of Gratitude.

4.   David O. Selznick. Once married to actress Jennifer Jones, Selznick produced the film *Gone with the Wind.* He died of a heart attack in 1965 at age 63. End of the Sanctuary of Trust.

5.   Carole Lombard. Three years after her marriage to Clark Gable, Lombard was killed when the plane she was on crashed into Table Rock Mountain outside of Las Vegas in 1942. Carole's will requested that she be buried in a white gown designed by Irene and placed in a modestly priced grave. Her simple crypt is in the Sanctuary of Trust next to Clark Gable. She was 34. Her mother, Elizabeth Peters, who was also killed in the crash, lies on her right.

6.   Clark Gable. Gable's marriage to Carole Lombard was the happiest in Hollywood, "a match made in heaven." When Gable died of a heart attack in 1960, at age 59, he was laid to rest next to Lombard. He was entombed wearing the blue suit that he wore when he married his last wife, Kay Gable, his gold wedding ring, his St. Jude medal, and the last Christmas gifts given to him by his two step-children. Gable's only child, John Clark Gable, was born in the same hospital where his famous father had died just 124 days earlier.

Gable & Lombard lie side by side in simple wall crypts.

7.   Sid Grauman. Grauman owned the Hollywood Chinese Theatre. His private mausoleum is in the Sanctuary of Benediction.

8.   Marie Dressler. Dressler won an Academy Award in the 1930 film *Min and Bill.* She is best remembered for her role of *Tugboat Annie.* She died of cancer in 1934 at age 64.

GLENDALE

FOREST LAWN CEMETERY

THE GREAT MAUSOLEUM

Jean Harlow's tomb in Forest Lawn.

9. Alexander Pantages. Pantages built the Pantages Theatre in Hollywood. His crypt is in the Sanctuary of Benediction.

10. Hollywood's Boy Genius. Irving Thalberg was 20 years old when he became production head at Universal Studios in 1919. He died of pneumonia in 1936 at age 37. His mausoleum cost $50,000.

11. Jean Harlow Buried in Gown from Libeled Lady. Known as the "Blonde Bombshell," Jean Harlow was one of the most popular actresses in Hollywood in the 1930s. When she died in 1937 of uremic poisoning at age 26, she was buried here in a gown of pink mousseline de soie, trimmed in hand-painted roses, daisies and bluebirds. It was the gown she had worn in the 1936 movie *Libeled Lady*. In her half-closed hand, she held a single white gardenia with an unsigned note attached to its stem that read: "Good night, my dearest darling." Speculation was that it had been placed there by her fiance, actor William Powell. Her bronze casket with a reproduction of her signature on its silver nameplate, was covered with 1,500 lilies of the valley and 500 gardenias. She was entombed in the "Jean Harlow" room which was lined with multicolored marble from France, Italy and Spain. The beautiful room was purchased by Powell for $25,000 as a shrine to the girl he loved. For many years he had white roses placed on Harlow's crypt every day. Powell is buried near Palm Springs.

12. Theda Bara. A silent screen actress, Theda Bara was the first to be called a "Vamp." She died of cancer in 1965 at age 65. Her ashes are in the left wall of the Columbarian of Memory near the front.

13. Comedian Jack Carson. Carson, 52, died of cancer in 1963. His ashes are in the left wall of the Columbarian near the middle.

BURBANK

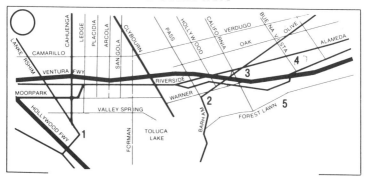

1.   Hollywood's Largest Studio. Universal Studio was formerly a chicken ranch when Carl Laemmle built it in 1915. In 1946 it was called Universal-International after it merged with International Films. It became Universal Studios in 1959 when the MCA Corporation purchased the 420-acre lot. 3900 Lankersheim Blvd.

2.   Burbank Studios. Built in 1926 as the First National Studios, the lot was purchased in 1929 by the Warner brothers. In 1967, the studio was acquired by Seven Arts Productions. The Kinney National Services took over the studio in 1969. In 1972, Columbia moved onto the Warner property. Humphrey Bogart, James Cagney, Bette Davis, Errol Flynn, and George Raft made their films here. The studio is now known as the Burbank Studios. 4000 Warner Blvd.

3.   NBC Studios. 3000 W. Alameda Ave.

4.   Disney Studios. Walt Disney built his studios here in 1939 on 51 acres that he purchased for $100,000. 500 S. Buena Vista St.

5.   Forest Lawn Hollywood Hills Cemetery. Lucille Ball, Liberace and Stan Laurel are buried here. 6300 Forest Lawn Dr.

Final resting place of Liberace in the Hollywood Hills.

78

BURBANK

FOREST LAWN HOLLYWOOD HILLS CEMETERY

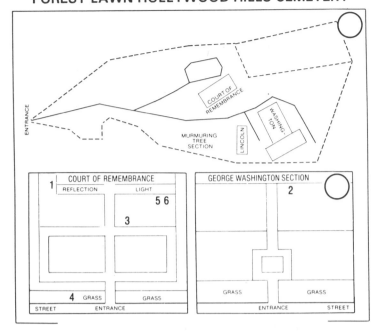

1. Lucille Ball. Lucille Ball Morton died of a ruptured abdominal aorta at age 77 on April 26, 1989. Cremated, her ashes are contained in a small cubicle in the middle of the wall on the right (about six feet from the floor) just inside the entrance of the Court of Radiant Dawn. Former husband Desi Arnaz, died December, 1987, in Delmar, California of lung cancer. He was 69.

2. Stan Laurel. The thin one of "Laurel & Hardy." Laurel died of a heart attack in 1965. He was 74. His headstone (mounted on the wall) is on the 2nd level behind the Washington statue.

3. Liberace. Born as Wladziu Valentino Liberace and known as music's most flamboyant showman, Liberace rests in a tomb embellished with his signature and grand piano, and located between two trees shaped like candelabras. The tomb also contains his mother and brother George. Liberace died in 1987 of AIDS.

4. Bette Davis. Davis died of cancer in 1989. She was 81. Her large crypt is in front of the wall, to the left of the entrance to the Court of Remembrance section. Davis' mother is also buried in the tomb.

5. George Raft. A star since his role as a tough guy/gangster in the 1932 film *Scarface,* Raft died in 1980 of respiratory problems at age 85. He lies in a simple crypt next to comedian Freddie Prinze.

6. Freddie Prinze. The former star of the TV series *Chico and the Man,* Prinze shot himself in 1977 (see page 55). He was 22. The nameplate on his grave has been stolen several times by the fans of the young comedian. His wall crypt is in the Sanctuary of Light.

STUDIO CITY

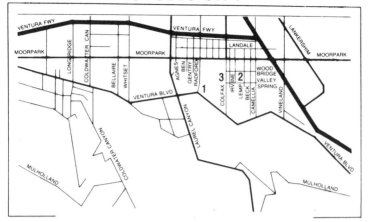

1. Republic Studios. The studio where John Wayne, Gene Autry and Roy Rogers made their western films was built in 1928 by Mack Sennett. The studio was sold in 1936 to Herbert J. Yates who renamed it Republic Studios. In 1963, CBS leased it, then purchased the 40-acre lot in 1967. It is now the CBS Studio Center. 4024 Radford.

2. "It" Girl Found Dead at Kitchen Table. In 1931, actress Peggy Shannon was hailed as another girl with "It." Fresh from Broadway where she was a Ziegfeld Follies beauty, Miss Shannon was brought to Hollywood as the hopeful successor to the "It" girl, Clara Bow. After several years of mediocre films, her career declined and she took to heavy drinking. In 1941, ten years after coming to Hollywood, Peggy

Peggy Shannon

was found slumped dead across the kitchen table here in her home. Discovered by her husband of seven months, her head was on her arms, a burned-out cigarette was still in her mouth, and an empty glass was beside her. She was 31 years old. Her death was reported to be from natural causes. Nineteen days after finding her lifeless body, her husband, Albert Roberts, joined Peggy in death when he put a 22 rifle to his head and killed himself. When police found him, he was sitting in the same chair where he had earlier

found the body of his wife, and just like Peggy, his head had fallen forward onto the same kitchen table. In a suicide note found near him, he wrote "I am very much in love with my wife, Peggy Shannon. In this spot she passed away, so in reverence to her, you will find me in the same spot." 4318 Irvine.

3. Bloomingdale Mistress Murdered with Baseball Bat. In 1970, beautiful 17-year-old Vicki Morgan became the mistress of department store heir Alfred Bloomingdale, 53. In 1983, she was beaten to death here with a baseball bat. 4171 Colfax.

TARZANA - ENCINO

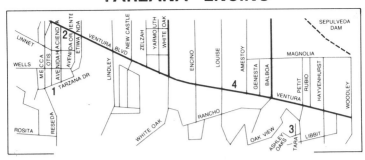

1. Ruins of Tarzan's "Tarzana." A huge, abandoned swimming pool sets on top of the hill. Water-gardens and fish ponds, once beautiful, are now overgrown with weeds. These, along with the foundations of former buildings are all that remain of the estate of Tarzan's creator, Edgar Rice Burroughs. The pool, built in 1913 by Harrison Gray Otis, founder of the Los Angeles Times, was the first ever constructed in the San Fernando Valley. Burroughs purchased Otis' "Mil Flores" in 1919 and renamed it "Tarzana." He founded the city of Tarzana in 1923. 18320 Tarzana Dr.

2. Tarzan Author Buried in Yard of Office on Ventura Blvd. When Edgar Rice Burroughs died in 1950 he left instructions that he be cremated and that his ashes be buried beside those of his mother's under the south side of the "big, black walnut tree" in the front yard of his office on Ventura Blvd. It was there in 1944 that he buried the ashes of his mother who had died in 1920. In a letter to his brother, Burroughs wrote: "cremation would be an easy way to get rid of me as any, and some part of my ashes would probably go up into the tree and would be no bother in the future for anyone." According to his wishes, his ashes were buried beside his mother under the tree that still shades his former office. 18354 Ventura Blvd. Tarzana.

Edgar Rice Burroughs buried under tree on Ventura Blvd.

ENCINO

Former home of Gable & Lombard.

3.   Gable & Lombard's "House of Two Gable's." In 1938, Gable and Lombard bought a 20-acre ranch here. Their two-story farmhouse with the gabled roof was called the "house of the two Gable's." After Lombard was killed in 1942, Gable lived in the home until his death in 1960. In 1973, his widow, Kay Gable, sold the ranch. Today, the house is surrounded by the "Gable Estates." 4543 Tara.

4.   Actor Kills Self in Hayloft. Handsome Ross Alexander was headed for stardom when his bride of four months killed herself in 1936 (see page 39). He remarried nine months later. Thirteen months after the death of his first wife, Alexander climbed into a barn hayloft here on his ranch, and like his first wife—he killed himself with the same rifle. He was 29. A restaurant is now on the site. 17221 Ventura.

SAN FERNANDO VALLEY

1.   Home of Manson Family. The Charles Manson gang lived here on the Spahn Ranch in the 1960s. 12000 Santa Susana Pass Rd.

2.   "Alfalfa" of "Our Gang" Killed Over $50. Carl "Alfalfa" Switzer of the Our Gang Comedies was shot and killed in 1959 during an argument over a $50 debt. He was 33. 10400 Columbus Ave.

LOST HOLLYWOOD

Since 1911 when the first movie was filmed locally in an orange grove, Hollywood has been known as the movie capital of the world. Eventually it earned the distinction of becoming the most famous city in the world. Among its residents were men and women whose influence helped shape the thoughts of America and the entire world. Over eight million persons visit Hollywood each year to see where these residents lived, worked and played. Many leave disappointed—much of what they had read or heard about had vanished. They found that dozens of Hollywood's priceless treasures and landmarks have been destroyed. The list below is only a portion of Hollywood's past that have vanished forever, and many are in constant danger of being bulldozed into more parking lots and mini malls.

Ambassador Hotel. 3400 Wilshire — Vacant, to be torn down.
Brown Derby. 1628 N. Vine — Parking lot.
Brown Derby. 9537 Wilshire — New development.
Columbia Drug Store. 6098 Sunset — New restaurant.
Disney Studios (first). 2719 Hyperion — Parking lot.
Dino's Lodge. 8524 Sunset — New development.
Don the Beachcomber. 1727 McCadden — Parking lot.
Fox Studios. 1428 N. Western — Parking lot/discount store.
Fox Studios. (back lot) 2000 Century Park East — Now Century City.
Garden Court Apartments. 7021 Hollywood — New development.
Garden of Allah. 8152 Sunset — Parking lot/bank.
Gilmore Field. 7750 Beverly — Small park.
Gilmore Stadium. 7800 Beverly — Parking lot/CBS.
Hollywood Canteen. 1451 Cahuenga — Parking lot.
Hollywood Hotel. 6811 Hollywood — Parking lot.
Hollywood Ranch Market. 1248 Vine — Mini mall.
Lasky-Demille Studios. 1520 Vine — Parking lot.
Lucey's Restaurant. 5444 Melrose — Parking lot.
Masquers Club. 1765 Sycamore — New development.
MGM (back Lots) 10202 Washington — Condominiums.
Mocambo. 8588 Sunset — Parking lot.
NBC Studios. 1500 Vine — Parking lot/bank.
Pan Pacific Auditorium. 7600 Beverly — Destroyed by fire.
Pickfair. 1143 Summit — Torn down.
Roach, Hal, Studios. 8822 Washington — Parking lot.
Sennett Studios. 1712 Glendale — Vacant lots.
Schwab's Drug Store. 8024 Sunset — New development.
Trocadero. 8610 Sunset — Parking lot.
Wallich's Music City. 1501 Vine — Mini mall.
Western Costume. 5335 Melrose — New Development.

MARILYN MONROE . . .

Follow Marilyn Monroe around the Los Angeles she knew, from the hospital where she was born, to the foster homes, orphanage, schools, apartments, to the home where she died and finally, to the tiny cemetery where she is buried.

1926 Born in Charity Ward. Norma Jean Mortensen was born to Gladys Baker Mortensen on June 1st in the charity ward of the Los Angeles General Hospital. 1200 So. State St. Los Angeles.

In Foster Home When 12 Days Old. Was placed in a foster home on June 13. 4201 W. 134th. Hawthorne.

Baptized in Four Square Church. Was six months old in November. 4503 W. Broadway, Hawthorne.

1927 Almost Killed by Grandmother. Was nearly suffocated with a pillow by grandmother Della Grainger here in July. 4244 W. 134th St. Hawthorne.

1931 Attends Kindergarten. Washington Elementary. 4339 W. 129th.

1932 Moves to Hollywood. With a new foster family, was enrolled in Vine St. School. 955 N. Vine.

1934 Attends Selma Street School. In third grade. 6611 Selma.

Mother Buys Home Near Bowl. With mother on Arbol St. in October.

1935 Mother Sent to Mental Asylum. Taken in by neighbors when mother was put into an insane asylum in February. 2062 N. Highland.

Placed in Orphanage. Put into Los Angeles Orphan's home in October. 815 N. El Centro.

1936 In Van Nuys Foster Home. With aunt Ana Lower. August. 6707 Odessa.

First time published photo of 1949 Marilyn the model.

Wins Track Awards. Won two first place track awards in jumping and running here at Lankershim School. 5250 Bakeman. North Hollywood.

Moves in with Mother's Best Friend. Moved in with Grace Goddard in December. 14753 Archwood, Van Nuys.

1937 Moves to West L.A. With Ana Lower again. 11348 Nebraska.

1938 Attends Sawtelle Elementary School. Here from September 1938 to June 1939. 1730 Corinth Ave., West L.A.

1939 Enters Junior High School. Attended Emerson Jr. High in September and graduated in June 1941. 1650 Selby, West L.A.

1941 Moves Back to Van Nuys. Was again taken in by her guardian Grace Goddard in July. 6707 Odessa, Van Nuys.

Meets Future Husband at Van Nuys High. Met her first husband Jim Dougherty here in September. 6535 Cedros.

First Date at Burbank War Plant Christmas Party. At 15, had first date with Jim Dougherty at the Adel Precision Products employee Christmas party. 231 So. Olive, Burbank.

1942 Moves to West L.A. With Ana Lower in January. 11348 Nebraska.

Attends University High School. 11800 Texas. West L.A.

Marries at Sixteen. Married James Dougherty in the home of friends on June 19th. 432 S. Bentley, West L.A.

FROM BIRTH TO GRAVE

1942 **Wedding Reception Held in Hollywood Night Club.** Celebrated wedding at Florentine Gardens. 5951 Hollywood Blvd.

First Home With New Husband. Moved into one-room apartment after wedding. 4524 Vista Del Monte, Sherman Oaks.

1943 **Moves in With In-Laws.** Lived with her husband's parents when he joined the service. 14747 Archwood, Van Nuys.

In New Apartment. June. Worked at Radio Plane defense plant while living here. 14668 Parthenia.

In New Apartment. December. 5254 Hermitage, North Hollywood.

1945 **Tries Suicide Twice.** Tried to kill herself by gas in April, and by pills in May. 5254 Hermitage St. No. Hollywood Blvd.

Moves in With Aunt. With Ana Lower. 11348 Nebraska, West L.A.

Becomes a Bleached Blonde. Had her hair bleached blonde for the first time at a beauty salon here. 6513 Hollywood.

1946 **Changes Name to Marilyn Monroe.** Took the name Marilyn Monroe in July when she signed with 20th Century Fox. 10100 Pico.

In Hollywood Studio Club. Room #307. August. 1215 N.Lodi.

1947 **Signs Fox Contract.** February 10.

Collects Unemployment. Filed in August after Fox let her go. Almost raped here by a prowler. 131 S. Avon, Burbank.

Lives With Actor John Carroll. With Carroll and his wife in December. 8491-99 Fountain Apt. #F, West Hollywood.

1948 **Under Contract to Columbia Studios.** Signed six-months contract with Columbia in March. 1438 Gower.

In Hollywood Studio Club. Room #334. 1215 N. Lodi.

Attempts Suicide. Tried suicide in September while living with drama coach Natasha Lytess after being dropped by Columbia. 1309 N. Harper.

1949 **Signs Contract With RKO Studio.** March 2.

Poses for Nude Calendar. Was paid $50 in May to pose for nude photos in studio of photographer Tom Kelley. 736 N. Seward.

Lives With 72-Year-Old Lover. With Joseph Schenck, co-founder of Fox Studios in July. 141 S. Carolwood, Holmby Hills.

1950 **Evicted From Home of 53-Year-Old Agent/Lover.** Lived with Johnny Hyde from October to December. 718 N. Palm.

1951 **With Shelly Winters Near Sunset Strip.** Shared an apartment with actress Shelly Winters in February. 8573 Holloway.

Signs Fox Contract. Signs 7-year contract in May.

In Beverly Hills With Drama Coach. Moved in again with her old friend, Natasha Lytess in December. 611 N. Crescent.

1952 **Blind Date with Joe DiMaggio.** Met DiMaggio on a blind date at the Villa Nova Restaurant in March. 9015 Sunset.

Places Mother in Sanitarium. Put her mother in the Rockhaven Sanitarium in August. 2713 Honolulu, Glendale.

Aunt Commits Suicide. Former guardian and her mother's best friend, Grace Goddard kills self in May.

1953 **Puts Handprints at Grauman's.** June 26. 6925 Hollywood Blvd.

1954 **Nine Month Marriage Spent in Beverly Hills.** Lived here with Joe DiMaggio from January to October. 508 N. Palm.

1956 **Married Arthur Miller.** Married in New York in July.

1961 **Divorced Arthur Miller.** Divorce granted in January.

1962 **In Hospital For Abortion?** Entered Cedars of Lebanon in July, reportedly to abort the child of Jack Kennedy. 8700 Beverly.

Dies of Overdose in Brentwood. August 5th. 12305 Fifth Helena Dr.

Buried in Westwood. Westwood Cemetery. 1218 Glendon.

THE MURDER SCENE

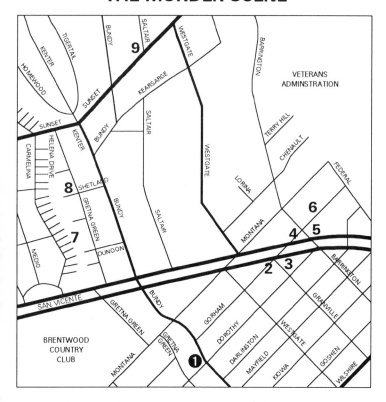

1. **The Murder Scene.** Nicole's condo. 875 So. Bundy.

2. **The Mezzaluna.** Goldman worked here and Nicole had her last dinner here. 11750 San Vicente.

3. **Ben & Jerry's Ice Cream Shop.** 11740 San Vicente.

4. **Starbucks.** Hangout for Nicole and Ron Goldman. 11707 San Vicente.

5. **California Pizza Kitchen.** Goldman was a waiter here before he went to work at the Mezzaluna. 11677 San Vicente.

6. **Ron Goldman's Apartment.** 11663 Gorham.

7. **Marilyn Monroe's Last Home.** 12305 5th Helena Drive.

8. **Nicole's 911 Call.** Nicole was living here on October 25, 1985 when O.J. broke her door down. 325 So. Greta Green.

9. **Nicole's Funeral.** Nicole's services were held here at the St. Martin of Tours Catholic Church. 11967 Sunset.

SIMPSON HOUSE

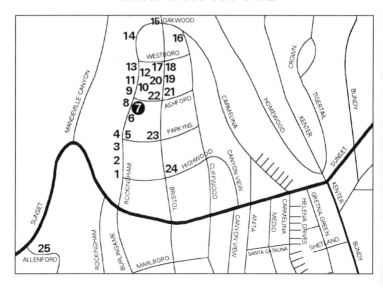

1. Shirley Temple and John Agar's home in 1951. 209 Rockingham.
2. Shirley Temple and her parents in 1941-50. 227 Rockingham.
3. Joel McCrea and his parents in 1928. 243 Rockingham.
4. Bette Davis, 1941. 301 Rockingham.
5. George Randolph Hearst, 1969. 318 Rockingham.
6. Rosa Lopez. The maid lived here for two years. 348 Rockingham.
7. **O.J. Simpson house. 360 Rockingham.**
8. Jean Arthur, 1939-41. 365 Rockingham.
9. Tyrone Power, 1946-47. 407 Rockingham
10. Cole Porter, 1944. 416 Rockingham.
11. Hume Cronyn and Jessica Tandy, 1947. 423 Rockingham.
12. Hal Roach Jr., 1949. 426 Rockingham.
13. Ed Wynn, 1954. 411 Rockingham.
14. Nigel Bruce, 1940-41. 521 Rockingham.
15. James Garner, 1995. 661 Oakmount.
16. Clifford Odets and actress Luise Ranier got married here in 1937. 543 Cliffwood.
17. Barbara Stanwyck in 1936. Jack Oakie in 1937. 441 Bristol
18. Johnny Weissmuller in 1940. Robert Preston in 1941. 436 Bristol.
19. Joan Crawford, 1930s-50s. Donald O'Conner, 1970s. 426 Bristol.
20. W.C. Fields and Errol Flynn came here for all-night drinking parties in the 1940s. 419 Bristol.
21. Hal Linden, 1986. 410 Bristol.
22. Telly Savalas in 1976. Tony Orlando in 1977. 409 Bristol.
23. Eric Von Stroheim, 1940. 307 Bristol.
24. Clark Gable, 1935. 220 Bristol.
25. Sydney Simpson's dance recital was held here at the Paul Revere School on the afternoon of the murders. 1450 Allenwood.

GRAVE OF NICOLE SIMPSON

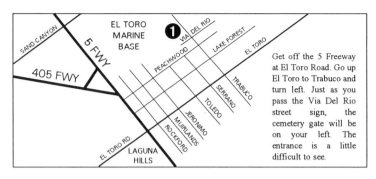

Get off the 5 Freeway at El Toro Road. Go up El Toro to Trabuco and turn left. Just as you pass the Via Del Rio street sign, the cemetery gate will be on your left. The entrance is a little difficult to see.

1. ASCENSION CEMETERY. Nicole Brown Simpson was buried here June 16, 1994. 24754 Trabuco Rd. in Lake Forest.

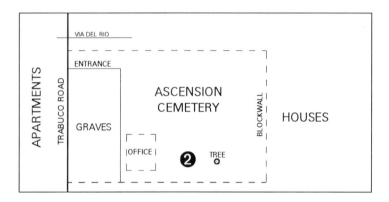

2. GRAVE OF NICOLE BROWN SIMPSON

After entering the gate of the cemetery, continue down the road and park near the office. Walk around the office until you are behind it.

While standing behind the office, align yourself with the tree as shown on the map.

Walk toward the block wall to the third row of headstones. Nicole lies next to her grandfather Josef Baur.

GRAVE SITES OF THE STARS

Adoree, Renee, 25
Alfalfa Switzer, 22
Allen, Gracie, 74

Ball, Lucille, 79
Bara, Theda, 77
Barbee, Cecil, 25
Bell, Rex, 74
Benny, Jack, 65
Berger, Elmer, 24
Beveridge, Daeida, 24
Blanc, Mel, 22
Bow, Clara, 74
Boyer, Charles, 63
Boyer. Michael, 63
Bushman, Francis X., 75

Calhern, Louis, 25
Carson, Jack, 77
Chandler, Harry, 22
Chandler, Marion Otis, 22
Clark, William Andrews, 20
Cohn, Harry, 21
Cole, Nat "King," 74
Cole, Cornelius, Sen., 21
Columbo, Russ, 75
Conte, Richard, 56
Crosby, Bing, 63
Crosby, Dixie, 63

Davies, Marion, 20
Davis, Bette, 79
Davis, Joan, 64
Davis, Sammy Jr., 73
DeMille, Cecil B., 21
Disney, Walt, 73
Dolly, Jenny, 75
Dolly, Rosie, 75
Dressler, Marie, 76

Eddy, Nelson, 21

Fairbanks, Douglas Sr., 21
Finch, Peter, 24
Fine, Larry, 75
Fleming, Victor, 25
Flynn, Errol, 73

Gable, Clark, 76
Gower, John T., 21
Grauman, Sid, 76
Greene, Lorne, 65
Griffith J. Griffith, 22

Hackett, Joan, 25
Harlow, Jean, 77
Hood, Darla, 25

Jolson, Al, 65
Jones, Spike, 64

Ladd, Alan, 74
LaMarr, Barbara, 24
Landon, Michael, 65
Lanza, Mario, 64
Lasky, Jesse, 25
Laurel, Stan, 79
Lehrman, Henry "Pathe," 21
Liberace, 79
Lombard, Carole, 76
Lorre, Peter, 24
Lugosi, Bela, 63

MacDonald, Jeanette, 74
Marx, Chico, 75
Marx, Gummo, 75
Mathis, Ruth, 24
McPherson, Aimee Semple, 73
Menjou, Adolph, 21
Monroe, Marilyn, 57

Otis, General Harrison Gray, 22
Otis, Marion Chandler, 22

Pantages, Alexander, 77
Powell, Eleanor, 24
Power, Tyrone, 20
Prinze, Freddie, 79

Raft, George, 79
Rappe, Virginia, 21
Rin-Tin-Tin, 55
Russell, Rosalind, 63

Selznick, David O., 76
Siegel, Bugsy, 22
Simpson, Nicole, 88
Stengel, Casey, 73
Switzer, Carl "Alfalfa," 22

Talmadge, Constance, 25
Talmadge, Norma, 25
Tanner, William Deane, 24
Tate, Sharon, 64
Taylor, William Desmond, 24
Thalberg, Irving, 77

Valentino, Rudolph, 23

Webb, Clifton, 25
Wilcox, Daeida Beveridge, 24
Wilcox, H. H., 24
Wood, Natalie, 56
Wrigley, Phillip K., 76

MURDER & SUICIDE SITES
OF THE STARS

INDEX

INDEX

INDEX

INDEX

INDEX

About the Author

Ken Schessler was captivated at an early age by movies and the stars that appeared in them. When he moved to the Los Angeles area from Chicago in 1954, he began to explore the city where movie studios were located and where many of the stars he watched as a youngster lived. It wasn't long before his interest grew into a serious research project. His desire to learn more of Hollywood's past took him to every street in Hollywood, and into hundreds of homes and buildings in Los Angeles, Hollywood, and Beverly Hills, gathering a tremendous amount of history and information that eventually led to the publishing of *THIS IS HOLLYWOOD*, which when first published in 1978, sparked a renewed interest in Hollywood that still continues today. His knowledge of Hollywood has earned him many TV and radio appearances as well as many speaking engagements. A former newspaperman, he lives in the Los Angeles area.